P9-DXN-042

Taking Sides

Taking Sides

A Speaking Text for Advanced and Intermediate Students

Teacher's Edition

Kevin B. King

Ann Arbor

THE UNIVERSITY OF MICHIGAN PRESS

Copyright © by the University of Michigan 1997
All rights reserved
ISBN 0-472-08422-4
Library of Congress Catalog Card No. 96-61011
Published in the United States of America by
The University of Michigan Press
Manufactured in the United States of America

2000   1999   1998   1997   4   3   2   1

No part of this publication may be reproduced, stored in a
retrieval system, or transmitted in any form or by any means,
electronic, mechanical, or otherwise, without the written
permission of the publisher.

Illustrated by William H. Bonney.

This book is for my mother, Margaret R. King.

Acknowledgments

Grateful acknowledgment is made to the following authors, publishers, and periodicals for permission to reprint previously published materials.

The National Court Reporters' Association for permission to use the twenty-six pieces in the *Humor in the Court* section (chap. 5) from the book *More Humor in the Court,* edited by Mary Louise Gilman (Vienna, VA: National Court Reporters' Association, 1984).

Sage Publications for many of the questions in the sections *Gender Attitudes (A Survey of Compatibility)* and *Marital Issues* (both of which appear in chap. 3), which derive from Mary Ann Fitzpatrick's book, *Between Husbands and Wives* (Thousand Oaks, CA: 1984). Copyright © 1984. Reprinted by permission of Sage Publications, Inc.

The articles "In Cairo, True Love Calls for Chandeliers on Top of the Head" and "Two Income Couples Are Making Changes at Work and at Home" are reprinted by permission of the *Wall Street Journal,* copyright 1996 Dow Jones & Company, Inc. All Rights Reserved Worldwide.

The sections *The Desert Dilemma* (chap. 2) and *Synergy (Lost at Sea)* (chap. 3) have been adapted from photocopied material in circulation a decade ago, the provenance of which has proved untraceable.

Experiments 5 and 6 in *Rationality (Sunk Costs)* were adapted from an example created by Amos Tversky and Daniel Kahneman in "The Framing of Decisions and the Psychology of Choice," *Science* 211 (January 30, 1981) and published by the American Association for the Advancement of Science, Washington, D.C.

Experiments 2, 3, and 4 in *Rationality (Sunk Costs)* were adapted from material created by Hal Arkes and Catherine Blumer in "The Psychology of Sunk Costs," *Organizational Behavior and Human Decision Processes* 35 (1985) and published by Academic Press, Orlando, FL.

The article *"Why Japanese Gourmands Will Die for a Taste of Fugu"* is reprinted courtesy of the *Boston Globe* 28 January 1992.

Every effort has been made to trace the ownership of all copyrighted materials in this book and to obtain permission for their use.

Contents

To the Student

The speaking exercises in this text allow you to discuss and debate a wide variety of serious topics. These are of general interest; however, they will also prepare you for many of the issues you will discuss or write about as you attend college. There is a lot of new *vocabulary*, and the most difficult words (which will be marked with asterisks) will appear in the "Vocabulary Gloss" sections, and many of the activities include writing assignments.

Although many of the new vocabulary words are defined for you, you will undoubtedly find some that you do not know. When this occurs, ask other students the meanings of these words. Use this opportunity to teach each other. You should also use the *context* to help understand unknown words. The section on *Paternalism* shows you how to do this.

In each section you will be asked questions that are designed to stimulate differences of opinion. In most cases, there is *no answer* that is clearly the *right one*. You can learn as much from one another as you can from simply listening to a teacher's opinion on an issue.

By doing the exercises included in each section, you will improve your problem-solving and critical-thinking abilities. You will also improve your negotiating skills and learn some concepts that are entirely new. You will learn to articulate your opinions on concepts you already know. You will learn a lot about American culture and about how your own culture's values differ from American values. You will learn something about the cultures of your classmates as well, especially in "The International View" sections, where you consider the topics entirely from your own perspective, taking the discussion in any direction you want.

You will also learn many *Conversation Cues*. These are words or phrases that we regularly use for speech functions like interrupting or disagreeing. Knowing some of these will make your conversation flow more smoothly and sound more like the conversation of a native speaker.

With a few exceptions, each unit *must be prepared at home, before class*. You will make your personal decision on an issue, or issues, and then you will share your decision with the class in general or with small groups of students. Finally, you will enjoy engaging in the debates that the exercises in this book will stimulate.

1

Introductory Exercise

Roommate Search

What are the most important characteristics for assessing the compatibility of a roommate?

Objectives

> to get to know your fellow students and their values better

> to see that different opinions on the same subject are valid and to be tolerated

> to practice the arts of compromise and consensus reaching

> to understand better your own priorities in finding a roommate

> to practice the skill of interviewing potential roommates

> to practice *Conversation Cues* for *Stating Opinions* and *Suggestion*

Introduction

If you study away from home, you will probably find yourself in the situation of trying to find a roommate to share the cost of an apartment. What are the most important characteristics for assessing the *compatibility** of a roommate? We will try to reach a consensus on this question. A *consensus* is a general agreement that not everyone will be in love with but that is a result of negotiation and compromise—it is the best decision that everyone can partially agree on. (Throughout this book, definitions of the words that are followed by asterisks will appear in the "Vocabulary Gloss" sections.)

Procedure

Part 1

Assume that you are single and are looking for one person to share a two-bedroom apartment. As a class, you will make suggestions for questions that you would ask a potential roommate. The teacher will then write each question as a category on the board. For example, if you would ask, "Do you smoke?" the teacher would write: *smoking*. When you have compiled a list of 12 to 15 items, look at the list and suggest omitting the least important or those that seem to be redundant. You will end up with a list of 10 items. A chart labeled *Roommate Search: Categories and Ranking* follows. Copy the ten items into the *Category* column of the chart.

Now, *individually,* you will rank the categories of questions according to their importance. (1) is the most important, (2) is the second most important, and so on, through (10), which is the least important. In other words, if you could ask only one question, which would it be? If it is, "Do you smoke?" then put the number 1 *to the right of* "Smoking" in the *Personal Ranking* column. If your most important question is, "Could you describe your *lifestyle**?" then put the number 1 *to the right of* "Lifestyle."

Next, you will meet in groups of three or four to make a consensus ranking. That means that the group as a whole must agree on the ranking. Put 1, 2, etc., for the group decision into the *Group Ranking* column.

Vocabulary Gloss

compatibility = getting along in a friendly manner
lifestyle = this includes things like having parties, having friends over, and preference for loud or soft music

Roommate Search: Categories and Ranking

Category	Personal Ranking	Group Ranking
_____	____	____
_____	____	____
_____	____	____
_____	____	____
_____	____	____
_____	____	____
_____	____	____
_____	____	____
_____	____	____
_____	____	____

Part 2

In different groups of four, three students will play the roles of roommates looking for a fourth roommate to take the place of one who just went back to France. You will decide who plays the fourth role—the potential roommate. Ask this person questions to determine whether he or she would be a suitable roommate. When you are done, report to the class as a whole about whether or not you found the student compatible.

Conversation Cues: Stating Opinions, Suggestion

Conversation cues are words or phrases that we regularly use for speech functions such as *interrupting, adding information, disagreeing,* and so forth. If these speech functions are our communicative strategies, then the *conversation cues* are the tactics that we use to accomplish these strategies. Using some of these conversation cues will make your conversation proceed more smoothly and sound more like the conversation of a native speaker. In this unit, we will concentrate on cues for stating opinions and for suggestion. The list of cues will be short, and you already know some, if not many, of them, so we will concentrate on those that are either idiomatic or used very frequently. Using these cues is not the primary focus of the unit, and you should not let the use of them interfere with your normal conversation. Further, the use of these conversation cues should not be limited to this particular unit. Use them from now on whenever you speak English. You should not feel obliged to use all of them during your discussion, but you should either keep your book open to this page or write the cues on a separate piece of paper and then put a check mark next to a cue each time you use it. At the end of the discussion the teacher will ask you how many times you used these cues. You might be the day's "cue champion."

Stating Opinions

(Use these to begin your opinion.)

> Basically, . . .
>
> To my mind, . . .
>
> As far as I can tell, . . .
>
> I'm afraid that, . . .
>
> By and large, . . .
>
> As a rule, . . .

Notes

"Basically" is a very popular expression. People use it to refer to the heart of an issue.

> *Example:* Basically, what you are saying is that Clinton will never be
> reelected, right?

"I'm afraid that" is also very common and really does not have anything to do with fear. It is just a polite way to begin.

> *Example:* I'm afraid that I don't follow you.

"By and large" and "as a rule" refer to the general case.

> *Example:* *By and large,* students prefer open book exams to essay tests.
> And *as a rule,* students who prepare thoroughly perform better
> on tests than students who do not read the course materials.

Suggestion

How about . . .

Examples: *How about* getting a new roommate?
How about this: we ask for a rent reduction.

The International View

Discuss the concept of "roommate" in your country. Here are some sample questions to help you begin your discussion.

Do people tend to live at home and not have roommates?

What considerations, besides the ones in the list that you used earlier
would be important for finding a suitable roommate in your country?

2

Ethics

Coercion/Paternalism

Objectives

to understand the libertarian philosophy of John Stuart Mill

to understand that while we all want to believe in the concept of "individual liberty" to a strong degree, we sometimes actually place severe restrictions on this concept

to show that philosophical issues pertain to our everyday lives

to see how abstract concepts are tested on the hard edge of reality

to learn to guess the meanings of unknown words

Introduction

Coercion is *forcing someone to do something against his or her will.* Coercion may be for a good purpose or a bad purpose, and coercion may be legal or illegal. For instance, a parent may coerce his or her child to eat her spinach, which we assume is a good purpose. A father may coerce a sickly boy to play football in spite of the child's inability to do well and his constant injuries, which we assume is bad.

We also encounter the interesting question of whether or not coercion can lead to good behavior. Some think that a person cannot be coerced into goodness. But a child might pick up his or her daddy's gun and say, "If you two don't stop fighting, I'm going to blow my brains out." And a parent might say to a child, "Be nice to your baby brother or I'll hit you."

Even when used for a bad purpose, coercion may be legal. A parent can be a perfectly cruel *tyrant** (just for the pleasure of dominating the children) and get away with it. Or coercion can be for a good purpose but illegal. (Feel free to disagree with this.) For example, during a famine, a rich man might buy up all the bread. Jean le Cric orders the rich man, at gunpoint, to give away all the bread. This is coercion, illegal but for a good purpose.

6

At any rate, coercion is a fascinating and troublesome issue. And one of the most difficult issues related to coercion is *paternalism*. This is the name given to the *state's deciding for the citizens what is good for the citizens*. This obviously *infringes on** individual liberty. And to the extent that we believe in that liberty, we will disapprove of paternalism. But in fact, most of us believe in some degree of paternalism, as we shall see.

But let's give *individual liberty* its fair say. The foremost spokesman for this doctrine is John Stuart Mill, who wrote about the subject in a book entitled *On Liberty* in 1859. Mill was concerned about the tyranny of the majority. Any time people join together to form a state, they give up some of their rights to the state. Drawing the line between individual and state rights is a difficult task, but it is important because the state is much more powerful than the individual and it can abuse its power.

Mill puts the case for individual liberty very strongly.

> . . . the sole end for which mankind are warranted, individually or collectively, in interfering with the liberty of action of any of their number is self-protection. That the only purpose for which power can be rightfully exercised over any member of a civilized community, against his own will, is to prevent harm to others. His own good, either physical or moral, is not a sufficient *warrant*.* (italics added)

Mill contends that a person cannot be coerced to do something because it will make him happier, wiser, or better or even because it is the right thing to do. You can argue with and reason with the person, but you cannot coerce him or her. "Over himself, over his own body and mind, the individual is *sovereign*,*" says Mill.

Do you believe Mill's thesis? Keep his arguments in mind as we investigate specific cases of paternalism. If you believe in Mill 100%, you can call yourself a "libertarian."

Vocabulary Gloss

tyrant	=	ruler with complete power, brutal and oppressive
infringe on	=	interfere with a right or privilege
warrant	=	permit
sovereign	=	self-governing
bungee jumping	=	jumping from great height with elastic (bungee) cords attached to one's ankles

Vocabulary Learning Technique

Throughout this book you will find "Vocabulary Gloss" sections in which the most difficult words will be defined for you. These will enable you to prepare your homework efficiently. However, there will always be other words in the readings that you do not know. When this occurs, instead of looking up every word in the dictionary, you should try to guess the meanings of the words from the context. You will often find that you can guess with a strong degree of confidence. Of course, you can never be totally sure that you are correct, but proceeding with a certain level of confidence—which you must determine for yourself—will allow you to work much faster.

For example, let's assume you do not know the word *humongous*.

Suppose that you encounter the sentence, "An elephant is a *humongous* animal." What meaning would you guess for this word?

If you guessed "very big" you would be correct.

Now let's look at a word that appears in the context of this unit. In the "Procedure" section that follows you will read the following scenario: "Suppose a man decides to jump out of a window believing that he will float upward. You reason with him unsuccessfully. Will you *restrain* him physically?"

Perhaps you do not understand the word *restrain*. Could you guess its meaning? What words could we substitute for *restrain* that would make sense?

Push? Shoot? Talk? Stop? Prevent? Hold?

If you thought any of the last three, *stop, prevent,* or *hold,* you would be correct enough. You would not need to look up the word.

Once you learn to trust your own reasonable guesses from context, your reading will go much faster.

Procedure

Read the following, think about the cases, then write your opinion in the space that follows. In class, one student will read each scenario, and you will be asked to read or speak your opinion. You will be expected to defend your position with logical arguments.

1. Suppose a man decides to jump out of a window believing that he will float upward. You reason with him unsuccessfully. Will you restrain him physically? If so you are acting paternalistically.
   (Write your answer here.)

Introduction to Question 2
Gerald Dworkin, a philosopher, thinks paternalism is justified in some cases—when it preserves for the individual his ability to carry out his own decisions rationally in the future.

2. Suppose you encounter an old man who is in constant pain both from cancer and from a half dozen diseases connected with old age. He tells you very lucidly that he wishes to commit suicide by swallowing an overdose of sleeping pills. If you stop him, you will preserve his ability to make rational choices in the future. Will you stop him?
    (Write your answer here.)

Introduction to Questions 3–5
Norman Daniels, another philosopher, thinks that paternalism is justified in cases where: (1) *competency* for rational action is missing, or (2) *voluntariness* is missing. In other words, if the state decides you are not acting rationally, they can restrain you. And if the state feels that you are somehow being coerced to do something, they can restrict your liberty to do it.

Others think that the state should act to prevent people from endangering themselves. But then the state would have to ban any number of activities. *Should the State Ban the Following?* (Add to the list any topic you think would fit and ask the group for their opinions on it.)

3. *Bungee jumping*°
    (Write your answer here.)

4. Boxing
    (Write your answer here.)

5. Eating blowfish (*fugu*) in Japan. (Read the article that follows
    and study the vocabulary that precedes the article. Because this
    is a reprint of an actual article, you will not find asterisks next
    to the vocabulary words.)
    (Write your answer here.)

Should the state ban bungee jumping?

Vocabulary Gloss

gourmand	=	person who loves good food
innocuous	=	not likely to offend or harm
penchant	=	tendency
knocked off	=	killed
stabbed	=	deliberately injured with a knife
dabbed	=	put one object lightly in contact with another (usually liquid or powder)
secretion	=	product (usually liquid) released by the body of an organism

flop	=	swing, bounce, or fall clumsily
goner	=	person or animal soon to die
numbness	=	inability to feel; insensitivity to pain or pleasure
lethal	=	deadly
Russian roulette	=	dangerous *game* of putting one bullet in a gun and firing at your head with 1/6 chance of killing yourself
toxic	=	poisonous
relented	=	became less severe
sliver	=	small, thin piece
set. . . back	=	cost (verb)
hauled	=	pulled, carried
plump	=	slightly fat
fare	=	something to eat
wriggling	=	moving like a snake
banned	=	prohibited
realm	=	kingdom; area under king's control

Why Japanese gourmands will die for a taste of fugu

By Colin Nickerson
GLOBE STAFF

Shimonoseki, Japan – Rank has its privileges, but the emperor and empress of Japan are denied one privilege that many Japanese consider a gastronomic birthright: the eating of fugu.

Fuss and fume though their highnesses may, the haughty chamberlains responsible for running the royal household decreed years ago that the innocuous-looking fugu—also known as globefish—is fare unfit for the imperial palate.

It is not a matter of taste, but of poison.

The intestines, liver and sexual organs of the fugu, a Japanese delicacy, contain tetrodotoxin, a paralyzing substance reckoned to be 500 times more deadly than cyanide.

The Japanese taste for raw seafood is well known; their penchant for fugu is incomprehensible.

This is the fish, after all, that nearly knocked off James Bond. In the final scene of Ian Fleming's novel "From Russia, With Love," Agent 007 is stabbed with a stiletto dabbed with secretions from the ovaries of a Japanese globefish, and instantly flops to the floor, an apparent goner. (Fortunately for Britannia, Bond was revived in the opening pages of the sequel, "Dr. No.")

The real world, alas is not so kind. On average, 100 Japanese a year are severely poisoned after indulging in this piscine favorite. About 30 die.

The most famous victim was Mitsugoro Bando, a Kabuki actor so revered that the government had designated him a Living National Treasure.

In January 1975, Bando swaggered into his favorite fugu restaurant in Kyoto and demanded a serving of sliced raw fugu liver. If the liver is washed and eaten in small quantities, the remnant toxin "produces a delightful sense of numbness of the mouth and extremities," according to a food column that appeared in the Yomiuri Shimbun, Japan's largest newspaper.

Delightful numbness notwithstanding, licensed fugu chefs are forbidden by law from serving the liver or other lethal portions of the globefish, no matter how much the paying public might clamor to play Nippon's version of Russian roulette. But this was no ordinary bon vivant. This was a genuine,

Reprinted from the *Boston Globe* 28 January 1992.

in-the-flesh Living National Treasure, feeling very "nihon teki"—full of true Japanese spirit—what was more Japanese than a platter of toxic fish organs.

The chef relented. Bando tweezered sliver after sliver of fugu liver into his mouth with chopsticks. "Heavenly!" he declared. He then died horribly of convulsions followed by respiratory paralysis.

One might think the Japanese would take the actor's sad fate as an object lesson and leave the fugu to flipper happily unhindered through the deep.

But no.

"Japanese have a gambling spirit and enjoy good fish," said Hideyo Kimura, a city official in Shimonoseki, whose fishing fleet harvests 90 percent of the 2,200 tons of fugu that the Japanese consume annually. "People regard eating fugu as very sophisticated, very glamorous."

And they pay handsomely for their piscivorous treat.

A single serving of fugu sashimi, or raw fugu—the flesh sliced to paper-thin translucence and then artfully arranged in the shape of a flower or a crane—will set the gourmand back about $250. Fugu is also served in a sort of stew or as deep-fried tempura. "Eating fugu is a sort of extreme of the Japanese culture," said Tomoaki Nakao, director of the Shimonoseki Karato Uoichiba Co. Ltd.,

a huge wholesaler and retailer of fish, crabs, mollusks, squid, octopi and nearly every other underwater creature. Including, of course, fugu.

"There are more than 22 edible species of globefish," he said. "The more poisonous, the more popular."

Most poisonous and, thus, most prized of all is torafugu, or tigerfish, named for its distinctive orange stripes. Many is the bold diner who has tasted of the tora, smacked his lips in satisfaction, and then heaved a startled gasp, eyes rolling backward, chopsticks slipping from numbed hand.

The globefish species most avidly eaten by the Japanese are caught in the Yellow Sea and the East China Sea, as well as in waters around the southern island of Kyushu. Catching the fish is hazardous in itself.

"Shimonoseki fishermen catch nearly all Japan's fugu because only the fishermen of Shimonoseki are brave enough," said Akito Kamita, who, not surprisingly, is a fisherman of Shimonoseki. The city of 260,000 inhabitants is located on the Kanmon Strait between Kyushu and the main Japanese island of Honshu.

Fugu are snared on long lines rigged with hundreds of hooks and then hauled aboard and removed from the barb by hand. Fishermen have died after being pricked by a hook that has pierced a poisonous part of the fugu.

A Tokyo Central Fish Market employee holds up a tiger blowfish *(fugu)*, whose internal organs contain a poison 25 times more deadly than cyanide. The nonpoisonous flesh of the *fugu* is prized as a delicacy by the Japanese. (REUTERS/Susumu Takahashi/ Archive photos. ID# 8800018.)

"Globefish are most popular to eat in January because the new year makes people feel expansive and lucky," Nakao said.

Sanpei Hiraoka, director of public health in Shimonoseki, insisted that eating fugu is perfectly safe—provided the chef is properly licensed and trained. Before earning the right to prepare and serve fugu without supervision, an aspiring fugu chef must undergo a three-year apprenticeship and then pass a rigorous series of tests and written examinations.

"It is almost like being a doctor, only we perform just one operation," said Kazuo Sasaki as he deftly excised the poisonous innards of a plump torafugu before turning the razor-sharp "hocho" blade to the sexual organs.

For the Japanese, fugu is not mere seafood to be consumed with no more thought than one might give to such ho-hum pedestrian fare as dried salt squid, wriggling live shrimp—called dancing ebi—or bright orange gobs of raw sea urchin roe.

"Eating fugu is an act of passion," Nakao said.

Indeed, fugu has seized the imagination of Japanese poets for centuries, although the traditional haiku and senryu versus inspired by the globefish tend toward the gloomy. As in Yosa Buson's celebrated poem of love lost:

I cannot see her tonight,
I have to give her up,
So I will eat fugu.

Once the eating of fugu was a crime in Japan. In 1590, the warlord Hideyoshi Toyotomi, enraged when his plans to do battle with a rival daimio had to be postponed after large numbers of his samurai died or became severely ill from feasting on fugu, banned consumption of the fish throughout the realm.

The edict was largely ignored, and by the mid-1600s the fish was popular among courtiers of the Tokugawa shogunate as well as sumo wrestlers, who asserted that when the fish did not kill it gave extra strength.

"Ever since the Edo period, fugu has been considered a gourmet dish even when it was technically illegal," said Kimura, whose office in the Shimonoseki municipal building is decorated with fugu balloons, fugu pottery, fugu ashtrays and posters depicting various species of fugu.

The legal ban was lifted in 1889. No one is certain why, although local legend has it that Prime Minister Hirobumi Ito paid a visit to Shimonoseki and was accidentally served globefish, which, law-abiding stalwart that he was, he had never before sampled.

"When informed the fish was fugu, the prime minister said that it was unforgivable that such a delicious taste should be prohibited," Kimura insisted. "So he ended the law, bringing great happiness to Japanese."

The International View

What similar things are banned in your country? What things are permitted that some people think should be banned?

Paternalism in Action: American Laws

Objectives

> to understand that an abstraction like paternalism has very real consequences, because it is translated into laws that have penalties for violation

> to build a consensus

> to understand better the political culture of the United States

> to understand and employ the *principle of charity* in persuasive writing and oral argument

Introduction

Here is a list of paternalistic laws that Americans disagree on. In most states of the United States these laws are in effect. But we do have a rebellious history. The state of Massachusetts nearly had a revolution when a law was passed requiring motorists to wear seat belts. The ordinary people rose up and, as in 1776, forced the law to be repealed. The majority of the people didn't want anybody to interfere with their right to choose, regardless of the fact that using seat belts was seen as a good thing.

Many states do require drivers and passengers in cars to wear seat belts. They argue that it costs about $5,000 more per accident victim for hospital care for people who did not wear seat belts than for those who did—an annual cost, per state, of about $10 million. This is paid by insurance companies, who pass on the costs to citizens by raising the price of insurance premiums. Of course, these states also cite statistics that show that seat belts save lives.

What do you think—*should we be required to wear seat belts in cars, or should that be the option of the people in the car?*

And what do you think of the 1996 vote of the California Assembly to repeal the mandatory motorcycle *helmet** law for people over twenty-one, saying that "it took the fun out of motorcycling"?

Vocabulary Gloss

helmet	=	head protection
consenting	=	agreeing
dueling	=	formal combat between two persons using weapons, with witnesses
fetus	=	unborn child
sued	=	asked to pay money for legal damages, like a fine

Procedure

Put a *check mark* in the appropriate space to indicate whether you *agree* or *disagree* with the laws. We will discuss these laws in small groups and try to reach a consensus. When your group has finished its discussion, write a *C* in either the agree column or the disagree column to note where the group consensus was. See the explanatory notes for questions 4, 5, 6, 7, 8, 9, 10 that follow this list.

Agree Disagree

1. ____ ____   laws requiring motorcyclists to wear safety helmets when driving

2. ____ ____   laws forbidding persons from swimming at a public beach when a lifeguard is not present

3. ____ ____   laws making suicide a crime

4. ____ ____   laws making it illegal for women to work at certain types of jobs

5. ____ ____   laws regulating certain kinds of sexual conduct among *consenting** adults in private

6. ____ ____   laws requiring a license to practice certain professions

7. ____ ____   laws that regulate the use of certain drugs that may harm the user but do not lead to antisocial conduct or crime

8. ____ ____   laws forcing people to save a specified portion of their income for retirement (American Social Security system)

9. ____ ____   laws forbidding certain kinds of gambling

10. ____ ____   laws regulating the maximum rates of interest for loans

11. ____ ____   laws against *dueling**

Notes

Question 4.   For instance, some companies forbid pregnant women to work where certain chemicals are present, for fear that damage could result to the *fetus** and they would be *sued.** But these jobs pay pretty well, so should the women be allowed to take the risk? A man can.

     Also, the U.S. Air Force, until recently, has forbidden women pilots from flying combat missions.

Question 5.   In other words, can two adults, of any sex, draw the curtains in their own house and have any kind of sex they want, or can some sexual practices be banned because they are considered immoral?

Question 6.   You have to have a license to practice medicine or law, for example. Can one person say to another person who is sick, "Look, I can make you better, and I will charge you one-tenth of what a doctor will charge, but you must understand I don't have a license."

Question 7.   Some people believe that marijuana, for instance, does not harm the user and does not cause him or her to rob other people to get money to buy it.

Question 8.   In the United States, approximately 8 percent of an employee's pay is automatically deducted and kept for his or her retirement. You don't have any choice in this. You cannot say, "I'll invest in my retirement fund by myself, thank you." If you never stop working, you never get any of your money back. And you get it in monthly payments, so you might recover only a small fraction of what you pay in before you die.

Question 9.   Betting on horse races is legal, and lotteries are run by the state. And you can gamble legally (roulette, card games, dice) in casinos in Las Vegas and Atlantic City and on some Native American reservations, but not elsewhere.

Question 10.   Loaning money at very high rates of interest (such as 50%) is called *loansharking*. Individuals who cannot get a loan from a bank often borrow money from *loansharks*—people who are willing to take a big risk and who may break your legs if you don't pay back on time. This money is often borrowed to pay for gambling debts (cf. note 9).

Writing Assignment

Choose one of the paternalism issues (1—11) and write your opinion in defense of paternalism or of individual liberty. This is a philosophical argument, so address the arguments of the other side with the *principle of charity* in mind. The principle of charity in a philosophical argument means that you consider only the strongest argument contrary to yours. If you can destroy the strongest opposing arguments the weaker ones will automatically fall. (Write one page.)

The International View

Are there laws in your country that you think are too paternalistic? Does your country lack laws that you think, paternalistically, should exist?

Does your country require the use of seat belts in cars?

JFK Memorial Hospital versus Heston

Objectives

to learn the facts of a case for retelling, as is done in law schools

to understand how a state supreme court decides a complicated case on paternalism and individual rights

Introduction

The following case was decided by the New Jersey Supreme Court. It is very relevant to the issue of "the right to die," which is much in the news. The case also deals with the very difficult issue of what to do when the right to practice one's own religion without government interference runs up against the right to life.

Vocabulary Gloss

ruptured   =   broken
spleen   =   organ near stomach
Jehovah's Witnesses =   a religious group
liability   =   (legal) responsibility

Procedure

As you read and reflect, keep in mind John Stuart Mill's thesis and the arguments for paternalism. Students will collaborate in retelling the story, making sure that no important details have been omitted. Then you will discuss the issue in small groups, each person giving his or her viewpoint. Finally, your teacher will tell you what the state supreme court decided.

JFK Memorial Hospital vs. Heston

Delores Heston, 22 and single, was severely injured in a car accident. At the hospital it was determined that she would die if not operated on for a *ruptured* spleen** and that she would die if blood transfusions were not given.

Delores and her parents were *Jehovah's Witnesses,** a religious group that forbids blood transfusions. She insisted that at the hospital she told doctors of her refusal to accept blood. But doctors and nurses said she was in shock. She was, or soon became, disoriented and incoherent.

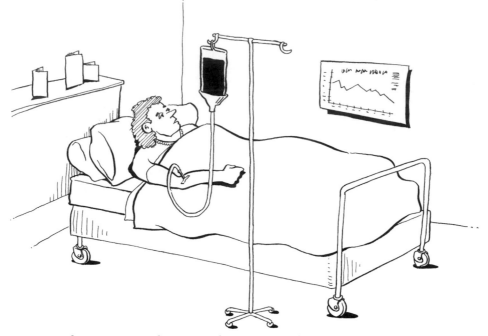

Can we force someone to have a transfusion in spite of the person's religious beliefs?

The hospital by law has to do all it can to save lives. If Delores had signed a release of *liability** for the hospital and the staff, the transfusions would not have been given. But she was unable to. Her mother did, however, sign a release. Her father could not be located.

The hospital asked the Superior Court to be appointed guardian for Delores, and the judge agreed. Now the hospital was free to give transfusions, without which they would not operate. They did, and Delores got well.

The case of Delores Heston is finished, so we can't argue about what to do there. However, the issue of forcing someone to have a transfusion to save his or her life is one we can discuss. Can we do this, in spite of the person's religious beliefs? Can we force a person not to let himself or herself die?

(Write a brief answer here. Your teacher may ask you to write a longer essay on this topic.)

The International View

How does your country deal with the rights of religious minorities? Do groups like Jehovah's Witnesses exist? Do they face similar problems?

The Desert Dilemma

Objectives

to make a decision that balances saving a life against the possibility of endangering others

to practice *Conversation Cues* for *Adding Information* and *Pointing out Irrelevancy*

Vocabulary Gloss

uninhabited = no one lives there
oasis = water source in the desert, with vegetation

Procedure

You will be divided into two groups. The teacher will read essentially the same story to each group, separately, but with slight differences. Group I will have some facts that Group II does not have and vice versa. You will hear the story twice. The first time you will just listen, to familiarize yourself with the story. The second time you will *take notes* (in English). This is not a dictation. Just take down the important information, as you would in taking notes in a lecture.

Next you will be assigned to small groups (preferably of four). Each group will have two people from Group I and two people from Group II.

Step 1
Retell the story, adding to the group's store of information. Make sure you have mentioned all the important facts and details. Use the *information adding* expressions that follow.

Step 2
As you retell the story, listen for irrelevancies. Point them out immediately upon hearing them. You will have a list of expressions to help you to do this. A lot of deliberately irrelevant information was included in the story. You may disagree over the relevancy of some fact. This is fine. If your teacher hears some irrelevancy that is not noticed, he or she may hint at it.

Step 3
When you have pieced together the entire story, you must decide what to do. Use the map that follows to help you. Remember that *one* of *you* is among the people on the expedition! Your life depends on your decision. Find out if anyone has experience with the desert.

When you have reached a tentative decision, your teacher will comment on it. You may then wish to reconsider your decision. Finally, when all groups have finished, each will briefly tell its decision, and the others will comment on it.

Conversation Cues

(Keep your book open to this page or write the cues on a separate piece of paper. Put a check mark next to a cue each time you use it.)

Adding Information

May I add that . . .

I'd like to add something; . . .

One more thing we need to consider is . . .

I think it's important to add that . . .

I think it's important for us to know that . . .

We also need to take into account that . . .

Let's not forget that . . .

Pointing out Irrelevancy

What does that have to do with it?

What does that have to do with our discussion?

What does that have to do with the topic?

I don't think that has anything to do with . . .

I don't think that is really related to . . .

How is that related to . . . ?

That really has nothing to do with what we're talking about.

I don't see how that fits into our discussion.

I fail to see the relevancy of_____ (that).

Is that really germane to our discussion?

Note
"Germane" means relevant.

Notes for "The Desert Dilemma"

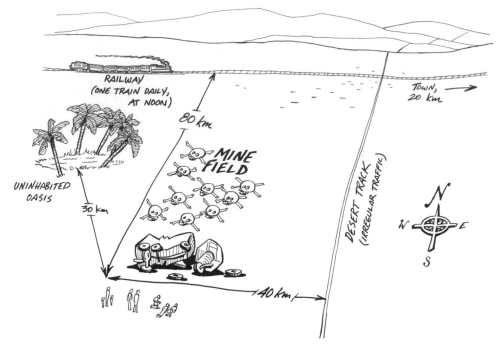

You are on an expedition to the Sahara desert.

The International View

Do you know of any cases of survival in extreme circumstances? What happened?

Health Care—Rationing

Objectives

to consider the ethical problem of rationing health care

writing a policy paper

Introduction

One of the problems encountered by any country that wishes to provide health care for its citizens is *rationing*. With a finite amount of money, we have to make choices on how to spend it. Do we limit the number of services we will pay for, or do we limit the number of people who can get the services?

This is a difficult and a sad choice, but an inevitable one. In England, for example, patients over 75 years old are denied *kidney dialysis*.* The reason given is that the treatment is ineffective for that population. In the United States, on the other hand, rationing health care services is widely considered immoral, so we ration people. For example, anyone under the governmental health plan can get kidney dialysis, regardless of age, but many people are not poor enough to qualify for the plan. In other words, we give unlimited treatment to a small number of people. Other countries give limited treatment to a large number of people. Which philosophy is better? Whatever you decide, some kind of rationing will exist. *In this unit, you will have to confront this difficult decision.*

For example, let's say you have $1 million left in your health budget. You could spend it on either of the following.

a. preventing death in 50 old people. This treatment would increase the quality of well-being (QWB) very little, and these people are expected to die within five years.

or

b. treatment for *acute* *arthritis* that would dramatically increase the QWB of 50,000 people and would last their lifetime (average age 45). Which would you choose?

(Circle *a* or *b*. We will discuss briefly in class. Of course, no one likes to make these kinds of choices, least of all politicians. We want to say *a and b.* So if you are unable to answer the question, that is OK.)

Vocabulary Gloss

kidney dialysis   =   removing impurities from blood when kidneys don't function properly (frequent treatment)

acute	=	severe
arthritis	=	inflammation of the joints
elderly	=	old people
indigent	=	very poor
longevity	=	length of life, long life
rabies	=	disease usually transmitted by bites (fatal if untreated)
drowned	=	died in water
cramp	=	painful contraction of muscle, sometimes paralyzing
vegetable	=	(slang) person in a coma
appendectomy	=	operation to remove appendix
resuscitation	=	being brought back from unconsciousness
updated	=	informed of latest news
cataracts	=	eye disease producing cloudy vision
maternity	=	pertaining to giving birth

Part 1. Values That Affect Health Care Rationing
We would like to have universal health care, but unfortunately we have limited funds. Thus, we need some criteria to help determine *who* and *what conditions* to treat.

Following is a list of commonly agreed-on social health values—that is, reasons for giving treatment—that we can use to help decide our priorities. To make sure you understand these health values, let's find an example of each one.

Match the *health value* with an example of it (a–f). Put the correct letter in the answer blank.

____   ability to function normally

____   cost-effectiveness or cost-ineffectiveness

____   length of life

____   quality of life

____   benefit to many as opposed to a few (value of system)

____   equality of service (value of system)

a.   expensive eye surgery allows me to see just 5% better
b.   *either* free immunization shots for all kids *or* artificial hearts for one hundred *elderly**
c.   artificial lung machine
d.   glasses
e.   guaranteed access to all citizens
f.   a wheelchair, medications

Part 2
Think of some other examples of goods or services that fall under the following health care values.

ability to function normally   _____

length of life   _____

quality of life   _____

Part 3. Ranking Treatments as a Part of Health Care Rationing
Let us now apply these health values to some scenarios to see how they affect our decision making in creating a universal health plan with necessary rationing.

Suppose you (the class) are a committee charged with making a recommendation for spending a small amount of money on some *indigent** patients. Your boss orders you to come up with a ranking of who should get treatment. You know there is not enough money for treatment of all of the patients. You also know that the doctors and hospital staff in this place are underpaid and are angry about it; they will not work unless they get paid. Sad but true.

First your boss asks you a question: "We have two possible criteria for providing treatment. Which should we choose?"

a.   Should we treat whoever walked (or was carried) through the door first?

or

b.   Should we decide according to the benefit of the treatment (e.g., the person at the front of the line has a stomachache and the last person in line is bleeding badly, so treating the last person has more benefit)?

(Choose a or b, then discuss in class.)

Now the boss says, "Proceed on the basis that I have decided on *b*. Here is a list of patients demanding treatment. We do not have the funds to treat all of them today. Give me a prioritized treatment list. Who will be treated first, second, and so forth—put a number in the blank before the patient's name. I am not asking you to play God; I am just telling you that our minimal resources will prevent all from being treated. The taxpayers refuse to pay more money; they're already screaming about high taxes. Do your best and understand that the final decision rests with me. I have provided you with the *cost level* of each treatment [in brackets]. When you add up your total cost level, the costs must not exceed *13.*" (The total could be less, i.e., 12.) Put a check mark on the line indicating which patients you have chosen.

To help make your decision, ask yourself the following question: *What difference will treatment make, as opposed to no treatment?* (in terms of *longevity,** quality of life, ability to function normally*).

In class you will meet in groups of three or four and make a consensus decision on who will be treated. Then each group will write the names of those you have chosen for treatment on the board. We will compare your choices, and you will have a chance to comment on the other groups' choices and to defend your group's choices.

____ *Adam* was bitten by a dog that he says was normally very friendly. The dog's appearance makes him suspect that it may have *rabies.** The dog has run off. Adam is afraid he caught rabies from the dog, and he wants shots to cure it. He is thirteen and an illegal alien. *[cost level 1]*

____ *Betty* has just learned that she is pregnant. Betty is a cocaine addict. She is worried that the baby will be born addicted, and she wants to enter a drug treatment program to break her addiction. She has tried to do it herself and failed. The father-to-be of the child is unknown. She is sixteen. *[cost level 2]*

____ *Chad* is in a coma after having nearly *drowned.** He climbed the fence around someone's swimming pool one night and got a *cramp** while swimming. A lung infection has also set in. He needs very expensive treatment from a lung-bypass machine, and one doctor has guessed that he will probably be a *vegetable** even if he survives. The dramatic *resuscitation** of Chad was filmed by a TV crew and was seen by millions on the 7 o'clock news. The reporters said that they would keep the public *updated** on Chad's condition. He is twelve. *[cost level 5]*

____ *Dolores* has unclear vision due to cataracts and needs operations on both eyes. Her only pleasure in life, she says, is reading, and now she can't do that. If untreated, the *cataracts** could cause blindness. She is sixty-two. *[cost level 3]*

____ *Eulalia* needs kidney dialysis on a continuing basis or she will die. She is fifty. *[cost level 5]*

____ *Frank* has severe arthritis in his hands and wants drugs and physical therapy to control it. He makes his living by playing piano at cheap bars. He is forty. *[cost level 2]*

____ *Gary*, twenty-five, is blind and wants a seeing-eye dog. *[cost level 1]*

____ *Ida* has AIDS and wants a drug that will prolong her life by about five years. Without it, she'll die in six months. She is thirty-five and is the mother of two healthy children, two and four years old. *[cost level 2]*

____ *Humbert* has a broken hip (*the result of chasing after women—it is alleged*). With treatment, there is a 98% chance he'll have full recovery. Without treatment, there is a 90% chance that he will be unable to walk. He is sixty-one. *[cost level 3]*

____ *John* needs an *appendectomy.** He is ninety and has a life expectancy of one year if the operation is successful. *[cost level 3]*

Writing Assignment

Top executives must make policy decisions, and these can be very hard. Your assignment here is one of the hardest. Suppose that the United States is restructuring its health care system. You have enough money in the health care budget to care for the majority of patients, but not all. Some sort of rationing must occur. The president of the United States wants a policy to be distributed to all the hospitals in the country. You must write this policy. The president asks you, "How do we spend the fixed amount of health care money? How do we decide whom to spend it on? Shall we just give health care to everybody who wants it, then when all the money is gone, in maybe six months, close down the hospitals?" Using the speaking exercise you just did as a starting point, write a policy paper of approximately two pages.

One student in each group will *not* write this paper, for he or she is the *president*. The president will read all the papers and then will write comments to each of the students, telling the students what ideas appeared good and what each policy paper was lacking (if anything).

Health Care–Providing Services to Visible and Invisible Victims

Objectives

to consider cost-effectiveness for the health-care system in general

speech writing

persuasive speaking

Introduction

In our previous work we discussed cost-effectiveness for individual treatments but not for the system in general. However, this consideration is extremely important. For example, one of the best things a city can do to improve and insure the health of its citizens is to put in a water purification plant. This provides incalculable benefits in reducing pain and productivity loss from stomach viruses, hepatitis, diarrhea, and even cholera.

Ironically, cost-effectiveness is often ignored in the United States because the victims are *invisible*. It can be proven statistically that if we provide *maternity** care before, during, and after birth, many lives will be saved. But those who don't get this care are nameless, statistical victims. On the other hand, when a two year old gets stuck in a pipe and the national news networks cover the story, we will spend any amount to restore the child to health. We like to see ourselves as charitable people, and helping such a child reaffirms our social values. In addition, not spending the money might be political suicide for elected officials.

We will investigate this issue with a writing assignment based on the earlier case of Chad.

Chad climbed a fence around someone's swimming pool one night and got a cramp while swimming.

Chad is in a coma after having nearly drowned. He climbed the fence around someone's swimming pool one night and got a cramp while swimming. A lung infection has also set in. He needs very expensive treatment from a lung-bypass machine, and one doctor has guessed that he will probably be a vegetable even if he survives. The dramatic resuscitation of Chad was filmed by a TV crew and was seen by millions on the 7 o'clock news. The reporters said that they would keep the public updated on Chad's condition. He is twelve.

To this we will add a few details.

Chad must be transferred from Florida to Minneapolis, Minnesota, where they have the sophisticated ECHMO lung machine. The experts now say that at best

Chad will be severely impaired. His brain was cut off from oxygen for too long. But with life-support systems he could live a very long time, at tremendous expense. The state of Florida has already paid $10,000 to keep him alive.

Chad has been on the front page of many newspapers, and tomorrow the governor has a news conference in which it is certain that he will be asked what the state plans to do about Chad.

Because of budget problems, major cities have recently cut back the number of police and firefighters, and they have been asking for aid to hire them back. Revenues are down because the state is in a recession. The citizens elected this governor because he promised *no new taxes*. Minority groups have been asking the governor for $250,000 for maternity care and for free immunizations for poor people. The governor has been delaying on this for a year, not wanting to put the state further in debt. Keeping Chad alive will cost between $100,000 and $500,000.

Writing Assignment

You are a speechwriter and advisor to the governor, and you get paid a lot of money for what you do. The governor has asked you to write him a one-page speech on "What to do about Chad," which he will read at the news conference tomorrow. Write the speech.

Reading a Speech

Your teacher will choose three speeches that will be read by the authors in class. The rest of you will be divided into three groups, and each group will help one author prepare his or her reading. Make sure that the reader

1. has good pace (not too slow, not too fast)

2. pauses after some important lines

3. forcefully stresses the important words and phrases

4. looks up to make occasional eye contact

5. uses hand gestures and/or other body language

Judging will be based on *which speech would you choose if you were the governor?* The judge will be (in order of preference) either someone who is not a class member, a selected student not participating in the preparation, or the teacher.

Knowledge, Information, and Ethics in Relation to Insurance and Health Care

Objective

   to consider the influence of ethics on insurance and health care

Introduction

Alexander Pope wrote, "A little knowledge is a dangerous thing." He meant that "a lot of" knowledge is preferable. But in our information age perhaps that is not always so. We will now look at a few ethical problems that arise from our scientific and technological ability to learn much more about our health and to transmit this knowledge easily.

   For instance, not long ago the Boston Transit Authority learned that one of its bus drivers was illiterate—unable to read. He had successfully driven a bus for years (we don't know how he got his driver's license) without any problems. He was an outstanding employee. However, he was fired. Was this right?

   We will look at problems dealing with group and individual knowledge and try to decide what role knowledge and information should play in our decision making.

Procedure

Decide whether your answer is "yes" or "no" in each case, and put a check mark next to your choice. In class, in small groups you will compare answers and explain why you made your choices and why you think they are best. Because these are hard questions, you may have doubts about what you think best. If so, explain your doubts to the group.

1.   Men have more car accidents than women. Should men have to pay more in insurance premiums than women? This is sexual discrimination, but we already practice age discrimination in automobile insurance policies. If you are over 65 or under 21, you pay more simply by virtue of being young or old. But of course, insurance companies sometimes frame the issue differently, saying that there is a "discount" for those over 21 and under 65.
     Yes _____   No _____

2.   Women live longer than men. Should women receive a "discount" in life insurance? (The sooner you die, the sooner the company has to pay benefits.)
     Yes _____   No _____

3. I am a young man who likes skydiving, bungee jumping, whitewater canoeing, and a lot of other very dangerous activities. I seem to be addicted to risk, though I don't know why. The Cheathem Insurance Company does not want to sell me life insurance. Should they be forced to?
    Yes _____   No _____

4. My insurance company has learned that my parents smoked two packs of cigarettes a day apiece and that they both died of lung cancer at an early age. I don't smoke, but the insurance company wants either to exclude lung cancer from my policy or to make me pay 50% more to cover the risk. Should they be allowed to do this?
    Yes _____   No _____

5. My insurance company knows that I have a defect in a certain gene, which usually leads to cancer. I don't know how they got the information. They want to exclude cancer from my health insurance and from my life insurance or charge astronomically high premiums. Is this fair? (By the way, your father owns the insurance company!)
    Yes _____   No _____

The International View

How does your country deal with health care? Can poor people get free treatment? Does the system work well? Are people satisfied with it?

3

Psychology

Survey

Objectives

to establish a quantitative view of marriage in the United States

to interact with native speakers

to increase cross-cultural awareness

Introduction

In some courses, particularly psychology, you will be required to survey the population at large. You will be surprised at how often the quantitative facts are different from your expectations.

Vocabulary Gloss

sustain   =   to support the weight of, keep up
openness =   telling the truth, not hiding things

Procedure

Fill out the survey yourself. Then ask one to five native speakers these questions. Whenever possible, just read them the question and the list of responses. If their answers surprise you, ask them why they responded as they did. In class, the teacher will conduct an informal poll of responses, and you will have a chance to comment on what surprised you and on any situations in which things are much different in your country. *The teacher will give you the correct answers.*

1.   Between _____ of all Americans get married at least once.

   a.   90 and 95%
   b.   80 and 90%
   c.   70 and 80%

2. Within five years after a divorce, _____ Americans remarry.

    a. most
    b. about half of the
    c. few

3. _____ Americans marry more than twice.

    a. Many
    b. Few
    c. No

4. With regard to nonverbal behavior, _____ are better at reading facial expressions, and _____ are better at interpreting a spouse's tone of voice. [fill in with: *men* or *women*]

5. Self-disclosure (revealing one's feelings) is more important

    a. at the beginning of a relationship
    b. farther along in a relationship

6. Relationships are able to *sustain*° total *openness*° over long periods of time.

    a. yes
    b. no

7. *What Do American Couples Argue about*? Rate these items by putting a number, 1–5, over each of them. 1 means most; 5 means least. The teacher will give you the correct answers. Remember, you are considering American couples, and the ranking order will not necessarily be the same as in your country. When you have the answers, discuss with your teacher the differences and similarities in ranking order for different stages of marriage. (*Note:* Good communication will prevent your spouse from feeling and saying things like, "You don't talk to me enough" and "Why didn't you tell me that?")

    a. (early in marriage)

    relatives   money   sex   communication   jealousy

    b. (early parenthood)

    relatives   money   sex   communication   jealousy

    c. (later on—around 15 years to end)

    relatives   money   sex   communication   jealousy

8. How much time do married couples living together actually spend talking to each other per week?

    a.   less than $\frac{1}{2}$ hour
    b.   1 hour
    c.   5 hours
    d.   10 hours

9. What percentage of American families have dinner together (all present) regularly?

    a.   10%
    b.   33%
    c.   50%
    d.   75%

The International View

In your country, do couples argue about different issues from the ones given in this section? Would the order of what they argue most about be substantially different?

Marriage, Cross-Culturally

Objectives

> to clarify what marriage is
>
> to share cross-cultural perspectives on marriage and what a good spouse is

Introduction

Marriage is not only a topic you will explore in this chapter on psychology, but something you will all need at least to consider seriously. We will begin by sharing what we think marriage is about.

Procedure

Check the items that you agree with. In small groups we will discuss which you chose and which you did not choose and why. Space is left for you to add items that you think are important and that have been omitted. Mention these to your group.

Part 1. Marriage Is About

____ sharing as much time as possible together

____ romance

____ keeping separate identities, activities, and interests

____ sharing innermost feelings, both positive and negative

____ having a good time

____ a lifetime commitment

____ being faithful

____ _____

____ _____

____ _____

____ _____

Part 2. Characteristics of a Good Spouse

Procedure

The class will make suggestions to generate a list of 15 characteristics of a good spouse. "Spouse" does not refer to just wife or husband, but both! And the characteristics should not apply just to a spouse you want but to *all good spouses*. When the full list is on the board, you will copy it. Then you will meet in small groups and form a consensus list of the 10 most important characteristics of a good spouse. In other words, your group must decide to *eliminate five of the characteristics* that the class generated. Cross out the ones your group eliminates. If you are strongly opposed to a characteristic being on the list, you may insist that it be removed. The consensus list must be acceptable to everyone. When you are done, the groups should report to the class as a whole on which characteristics they eliminated. Other groups may comment on the choices.

Characteristics of a Good Spouse

_____

_____

_____

_____

_____

_____
_____
_____
_____
_____
_____
_____
_____
_____
_____

The International View

In your country, are there characteristics necessary for "a good wife" that are not applicable to "a good husband" and vice versa?

Gender Attitudes

Objectives

to understand the different conceptions of the roles of men and women in society that different cultures have

to understand how these conceptions can affect the viability of a marriage

to understand how the gender roles are changing in the changing world economy

Procedure

Part 1. "Two-Income Couples Are Making Changes at Work and at Home"

Read the article and answer the questions that follow. (Because this is a reprint of an actual article, you will not find asterisks next to the vocabulary words.)

Vocabulary Gloss

breadwinner	=	person who earns money
clout	=	power
tug	=	pull
toddler	=	young child (around two years old)
shun	=	avoid
passed up	=	declined
grooming (someone)	=	preparing, training someone
glass ceiling	=	deliberately undefined barrier to how high one can progress in company hierarchy
"face time"	=	amount of time one is visible at workplace

Work & Family

By Sue Shellenbarger

___

Two-Income Couples are Making Changes at Work and at Home

Think fast. What kind of American family is most represented in the work force?

a) "Traditional" couples with one male breadwinner

b) Dual-earner couples

c) Families headed by single men or women

If you answered dual earners, you're right. After steady growth for decades, nearly half of all workers, or 48%, come from married dual-earner couples, the Bureau of Labor Statistics estimates. Though many companies are still run as if Ozzie and Harriet were the mode, only 9.4% of workers come from so-called traditional families. By 2000, two-paycheck couples will rise to a majority, or 51%, of all families, from 41% in 1980, says economist Sandra Shaber of Wefa Group.

Though the trend isn't new, major changes in the nature of dual-earner couples are accompanying the growing numbers, catching many employers off guard. Women in dual-earner households are gaining in job status and earnings as they become more experienced in the workplace, giving them more clout at work and at home. And more of the men, often the product themselves of two-income households, have more egalitarian views of gender roles.

A new kind of "collaborative couple" is emerging as a result, says Rosalind Barnett, senior scholar at Radcliffe College's Murray Research Center and co-author with Caryl Rivers, a Boston University journalism professor, of a new book on dual earners due out in May. These pairs share parenting and appear to value each other's jobs more than traditional couples.

Partners' jobs buffer each other against layoffs and career changes and breaks. Their work and home lives are intertwined; what affects one partner on the job or at home affects the other, and neither makes career decisions in a vacuum.

"It's hard to overstate the importance of this change," Dr. Barnett says. "Men's and women's work and home lives are like a spider's interconnected web; a tug that occurs at one section of the web sends vibrations all through it." In this first of three columns on dual earners, here are a few ways this web is encompassing the workplace:

Men view their careers differently than they did in the past. Men increasingly see their careers in relation to their wives'. In a best-case scenario (assuming both have secure, well-paying jobs), the men are enjoying new freedom. Rod Schrock, a Harvard M.B.A. who heads Compaq Computer's Presario personal-computer unit, is a hard-charging manager known for working long hours. But he also is deeply involved with his toddler son, Jared, and is considering staying home for a while some time in the future.

His wife is a director of marketing in Compaq's portables division, and "since we both have good jobs we may end up trading places every other year or so," he says. "We have this argument: Who is going to get to stay home?"

___

Reprinted from the *Wall Street Journal* 14 Febuary 1996.

In another twist, more men are shunning traditional career paths. Executive development consultant Ed Betof has passed up promotions or enticing job offers four times, partly to avoid disrupting his wife's career. "We decided early on that her career and my career had exactly the same weight," he says. Such values can confound employers' plans. At a conference, a computer-company manager lamented that five employees, including two men in dual-earner marriages, had turned down promotions. If companies are grooming people for leadership posts they can't accept, "something is wrong," he said.

Dual-earner men hit their own glass ceiling. In a study of 348 married male managers with children at home, Linda Stroh of Loyola University in Chicago and Jeanne Brett of Northwestern University found those with employed spouses got pay raises totaling 59% in five years, less than the 70% raises given those with wives at home. Two possible explanations: Dual-earner men worked two fewer hours per week, on average, possibly violating unwritten "face time" rules; also, they lack stay-at-home wives who aid their careers by doing all the housework and entertaining co-workers.

Resistance to relocation hits new heights. A 1995 Atlas Van Lines survey of 147 employers found 82% had employees rejecting relocation offers in 1994, up from 68% in 1991. One reason may be that a hefty 64% of the employers offer no help for employees' spouses in finding jobs after a move. When one consumer-products company tried to relocate 300 men and women to the Midwest from the Northeast, 200 refused, mostly because of worries about spouses' jobs, says Richard Pinola, CEO of Right Management, Philadelphia human-resource consultants.

Rising demand for spousal assistance is most evident among M.B.A. recruits in their 20s, says Bev Berberich, relocation manager for S.C. Johnson Wax and president of the Employee Relocation Council, a non-profit group. Most come from dual-earner couples and "one of the first questions out of their mouths is, 'What are you going to do for my partner?' " she says.

Women's careers benefit from supportive husbands. Employers have long stereotyped single, childless women as model potential managers. But a new generation of dual earners may be starting to shatter that view. A 1993 study by researchers at Pace University and Rider College shows married women earning more than single women, perhaps, the study suggests, because of husbands' support for their careers.

Reading Questions

1. Which type of man tends to have more egalitarian views of gender roles?
    a. a man in a traditional marriage (one breadwinner)
    b. a man in a dual-earner marriage
    c. a single man with a child or children

2. A man is more likely now to take a better job if it means disrupting his wife's career.
    a. true
    b. false

3. "We decided early on that her career and my career had exactly the same *weight*." In this sentence, *weight* means
    a. number of kilograms
    b. importance
    c. time before starting

4. Men with working spouses get higher raises than those with wives who stay home.
   a. true
   b. false

5. Men with working wives hit a "glass ceiling" for which of these reasons?
   a. They work fewer hours, violating unwritten "face time" rules.
   b. Their wives don't aid their careers by entertaining co-workers.
   c. Both a and b.

6. More and more men are refusing to relocate because their companies refuse to help their spouses find new jobs.
   a. true
   b. false

7. Married women make more money than single women, on average.
   a. true
   b. false

Part 2. Gender Attitudes: A Compatibility Survey
(This exercise is to be done in a mixed-sex class.)

"Gender attitudes" refers to the attitudes that we have toward roles of a man or a woman in a culture. These attitudes are a good predictor of marital satisfaction. That is, if you and your partner have similar attitudes, you are more likely to be a happy couple. If you and your partner have very different attitudes, you are less likely to be a happy couple in the long run.

In this exercise you will compare your attitudes with those of a student (or students) of the opposite sex. Remember that sharing similar attitudes about important matters will help two people have a happy marriage.

Vocabulary Gloss

egalitarian	=	believing in equality
long range	=	for 10 or 20 years
achiever	=	person who earns the money, honors, makes a reputation
worse off	=	not doing so well (psychologically, physically, mentally)

Procedure

A list of questions follows that will be used to test your compatibility with a partner. For each question, circle the response that is closest to your own beliefs: *St. Ag.* = strongly agree; *Ag.* = agree; *Dis.* = disagree; *St. Dis.* = strongly disagree.

Compatibility Questions

1. A working mother can establish just as warm and secure a relationship with her children as a mother who does not work.
    St. Ag.   Ag.   Dis.   St. Dis.

2. Parents should encourage just as much independence in their daughters as in their sons.
    St. Ag.   Ag.   Dis.   St. Dis.

3. Men should share the housework, such as doing the dishes, cleaning, and so forth, with women.
    St. Ag.   Ag.   Dis.   St. Dis.

4. Men and women should be paid the same money if they do the same work.
    St. Ag.   Ag.   Dis.   St. Dis.

5. Women should be considered as seriously as men for jobs as executives or politicians or president.
    St. Ag.   Ag.   Dis.   St. Dis.

6. A man can make *long range** plans for his life, but a woman can deal only with day to day problems.
    St. Ag.   Ag.   Dis.   St. Dis.

7. It is more important for a wife to help her husband's career than to have a career herself.
    St. Ag.   Ag.   Dis.   St. Dis.

8. It is much better for everyone involved if the man is the *achiever** outside the home and the woman takes care of the home and family.
    St. Ag.   Ag.   Dis.   St. Dis.

9. A preschool child will probably be *worse off** if his or her mother works.
    St. Ag.   Ag.   Dis.   St. Dis.

10. Women who do not want at least one child are being selfish.
    St. Ag.   Ag.   Dis.   St. Dis.

Now, for each question, compare your choice with a partner of the opposite sex. (If there are unequal numbers of males and females, you may have to compare with two partners.) First, put a check mark to indicate your opinion under one of the four choices in the *Compatibility Rating* chart on p. 41. Then mark your partner's choice. Discuss the reasons for your decisions. Then, using the following guidelines, put a number (0–3) in the compatibility column of the *Compatibility Rating* chart.

a. If you and your partner have the same response, put *0*.

b. If your responses are adjacent (e.g., *strongly agree/agree,* or *agree/disagree,* or *disagree/strongly disagree*), put *1*.

c. If your responses are two apart, (e.g., *agree/strongly disagree*), put *2.*

d. If your responses are three apart (e.g., *strongly agree/strongly disagree*), put *3.*

When you finish discussing all the gender attitudes statements, total your compatibility score. The lower the score, the more compatible you and your partner are.

   As a group, you might want to find out who had the lowest and highest scores. You might also enjoy finding out how many *egalitarians* and how many *traditionalists* there are in your class. Is one sex more traditional than the other sex?

Compatibility Rating

Compatibility Number	*St. Ag.*	*Ag.*	*Dis.*	*St. Dis.*
1. _____	_____	_____	_____	_____
2. _____	_____	_____	_____	_____
3. _____	_____	_____	_____	_____
4. _____	_____	_____	_____	_____
5. _____	_____	_____	_____	_____
6. _____	_____	_____	_____	_____
7. _____	_____	_____	_____	_____
8. _____	_____	_____	_____	_____
9. _____	_____	_____	_____	_____
10. _____	_____	_____	_____	_____

Egalitarian _____   *Traditional* _____

Look at your own responses for numbers 1–5. If you agreed or strongly agreed with most of them, you are an *egalitarian*. Put a check mark in the box above.

Check your responses for numbers 6–10. If you agreed or strongly agreed with most of these, you are *traditional*. Put a check mark in the box above.

Gender and Power in Discussion

This exercise offers you an opportunity to do some brief but original psychological and linguistic research and to analyze and interpret raw data. The task is closely related to the issues you will take up in chapter 6, in the section *You Don't Understand Me!*

Many people feel that men and women communicate differently, and that they have different views of the purpose of communication—men seeing communication as a means of conveying information, and women seeing it as a way of creating emotional ties.

Your task here is to see if mixed groups of males and females communicate differently. Specifically, you will be looking at expressions of power and dominance. Do men or women try more to dominate a discussion?

There are many ways to approach this question, but we will have to settle for just a few indicators: *interruptions, tag questions,* and *challenges.*

The class will be divided into small mixed-sex groups (preferably two men and two women per group) to talk about the questions in "The International View" section. A student researcher will be assigned to each group. He or she will monitor the discussion and make a check mark on the list that follows each time that a woman or man uses one of these indicators. Then he or she will count the number of times that each sex used interruptions, tag questions, and challenges to see if there is a genuine difference between men and women in this class regarding these forms of communication. Each student researcher will then report his or her findings to the whole class.

Interruptions occur when one person starts speaking before another has finished talking. They tend to indicate an expression of power.

Tag questions are added to the end of a sentence ("don't you?" "doesn't she?" "do you?"). These tend to indicate unsureness and deference; in other words, an abdication of power.

Challenges are strong disagreements. Challenges can be in the form of questions. For instance, if I say that everybody should read this book, and you say, "Don't you think everybody should make up their own mind about what to read?" you are challenging me. Challenges are an assertion of power.

Interruptions
Men   _____   Total   _____
Women _____   Total   _____

Tag Questions
Men   _____   Total   _____
Women _____   Total   _____

Challenges
Men   _____   Total   _____
Women _____   Total   _____

The International View

Are couples becoming more or less egalitarian in your country? How? Why?

Women in America often hit a *glass ceiling* in large corporations. Only 5% of high management jobs are held by women. Is the situation similar in your country? Is there, instead, a *wooden ceiling*, a situation in which men are open about not wanting women at high levels? Or do many women have high management jobs?

Marital Issues

Objectives

to find out to what extent the class agrees on the issues of *ideology, interdependence,* and *communication* in marriage

to explore cross-cultural attitudes on these issues

to share wedding customs

Part 1. "In Cairo, True Love Calls for Chandeliers On Top of Head"

Read the article and be prepared to answer the discussion questions in class. (Because this is a reprint of an actual article, you will not find asterisks next to the vocabulary words.)

Vocabulary Gloss

chandelier	=	an elaborate lighting fixture hanging from the ceiling and comprising many bulbs
spring for	=	pay for
lavish	=	extravagant
opt for	=	choose
low-key	=	not extravagant, restrained
fuss	=	needless excitement

In Cairo, True Love Calls for Chandeliers On Top of the Head

It's Costly, Which is the Point; A Groom Works Two Jobs to Save for Wedding Bash

By Amy Dockser Marcus
Staff Reporter of the *Wall Street Journal*

CAIRO, Egypt—Azza Riad still believes that love conquers all. Sometimes it just takes a while.

The 24-year-old cosmetics saleswoman has been engaged for three years. She and her would-be groom want to set a wedding date. They just can't afford it.

In Egypt, romance doesn't come cheap. An aspiring Romeo is expected to come up with bride money and to provide a fully furnished apartment, spending tens of thousands of dollars before anyone even walks down the aisle. The wedding and reception—with the requisite singers, belly dancers, and food—cost a bundle, too.

But Ms. Riad's intended earns a monthly income of less then $150 working as an accountant in a clothing company. "He can barely afford to get a haircut," she sighs.

Bridal Path

No other event defines status and social standing in Egypt quite like a wedding. Many parents begin saving for the nuptials as soon as a child is born. Even so, in a country where per capita earning is only about $700 a year, many couples end up borrowing from relatives and even employers in order to keep up with the neighbors.

"Weddings have always been a way of showing off," says Madiha el-Safty, a professor of sociology at the American University of Cairo. "But soon, getting married is going to be beyond the means of any social class."

In a Cairo courtyard, a group of young Egyptian men talk about the social pressures that force them to spring for lavish affairs. "Women won't marry you unless you give them a lot of expensive jewelry, a big flat and lots of furniture," says Amr Saleh, 24, a technician who estimates it will take two years of working two jobs a day in order to save up for his wedding.

"Even when you get them to agree to a smaller wedding," adds his friend, Ahmed Mahmoud, "once their parents get involved, the pressure really begins."

Laser Love

Sitting in her office in downtown Cairo, one mother planning a wedding for her 30-something son says the couple initially vetoed the traditional belly dancers with chandeliers on their heads, the 30-piece band that accompanies the bride as she makes her grand entrance at the reception, and the chance to have their names flashed with lasers on the hall ceiling, opting instead for a more low-key affair in order to save money.

Reprinted from the *Wall Street Journal* 14 February 1996.

"But when the bride's parents heard about it, they got very upset," says the groom's mother, who asked not to be named because she doesn't want to insult her son's future in-laws. "They said the guests would start wondering why their daughter wasn't good enough for a real wedding. So we're going to make it fancy."

At the Dar al-Iwaa Islamic community center, Sheik Mohammed Abdel Salam doesn't see what the fuss is all about. At his mosque, needy couples receive cash grants to help pay for furniture and

Weddings at a Glance	
Average cost of an American Wedding	$8,000
Bride's attire	9%
Other attire	12%
Reception	33%
Other items	46%
Average wedding-dress cost	$670
Average number of sites visited to plan a wedding	30
Number of weddings in U.S. annually	2.3 million

Sources: U.S. Department of Vital Statistics. We Do Inc.

renting an apartment. The special "marriage-facilitating committee" will find part-time jobs at businesses owned by its followers for future grooms who need to earn extra money. And couples save on the reception, since belly dancers and singers are considered un-Islamic. (That's why many couples have the party at a hotel or social club.) Instead, newlyweds are encouraged to honeymoon in Mecca, Islam's holiest city, or for those with smaller budgets, tour Cairo's many mosques.

Sheik Salam does have some requirements for couples who want his help getting married. Women

aren't allowed to wear makeup and must agree to be veiled. Men must pray every day. "Romance fades," the sheik says about his strict criteria. "What counts is seriousness about being married."

Still, for many couples, the drive to finance a fancy wedding continues unabated. The government, in an effort to make it easier for young couples to marry, has started building 50,000 new apartments that will eventually be sold at below-market prices and with government-subsidized loans. And furniture stores, dress shops and wedding halls have all gotten into the act, offering couples 30-month pay-by-installment plans for all their marriage needs.

Sure, Nagih Abdel Raziq figures he can have three children in the time it will take to finish paying back the bills for the furniture he is looking at with his fiancee, but he says the financial sacrifice is worth it. "I'm happy that I'm getting married," says the 27-year-old engineer. "I won't settle for anything but the best."

That is a feeling that Cairo's better hotels are counting on. Magued El Leissy, catering sales manager at the Cairo Marriott Hotel, runs down the list of what the hotel can offer on the big day: a laser show, video cameras with a wide screen for watching the wedding unfold, balloon sculptures in the shape of a bride and groom, dancers, singers, eastern and western bands, and the hotel's famous nine-story wedding cake. "We used to bring the cake down from the ceiling on a mini-elevator," he says to a prospective client, "but we had to stop that because it turned out not to be so safe. Now we have it spring up from under a covered box."

During the peak season in the summer months, the top hotels usually host two weddings a day and couples are urged to book months in advance. The tab for all this luxury often runs as high as $30,000, but for many, that's a small price to pay for love. Besides, for the bride dreaming of making a grand entrance into married life, Mr. El Leissy says with enthusiasm, "We have the best staircase in town."

Discussion Questions

Discuss wedding customs in your country. Do weddings tend to be lavish affairs? Are there tricks played on the couple or on the bride or groom? In the United States, the average wedding costs $8,000. The price of the wedding dress averages $670. What are the average costs of these items in your country? Are they as high as in Cairo (where a lavish wedding can cost $30,000)?

What kind of wedding do you want to have (or did you have)?

Part 2. Ideology, Interdependence, and Communication Issues

There is a correlation of successful marriage and similar views on ideology, interdependence, and communication.

Procedure

Put a check mark in the blank indicating whether you agree *(Ag.)* or disagree *(Dis.)* with the following 16 statements. In class, groups of three or four will discuss each question. If you can reach a *majority* decision, put *(M)* next to that *majority* choice. The teacher will conduct an informal survey of group decisions.

	Ag.	Dis.

Ideology

1. A woman should take her husband's last name when she marries. ____ ____

2. My wedding ceremony will be (was) very important to me. ____ ____

3. In marriage, fidelity is not necessary. ____ ____

4. In the perfect relationship there is much laughing and doing of things spontaneously (as soon as they come to mind). ____ ____

Interdependence

5. It is important for a couple to tell each other how much they care about and love each other. ____ ____

6. When one spouse feels depressed or bad, the other spouse should comfort and reassure him or her. ____ ____

7. It is important for one to have some private space that is all his or her own and separate from the spouse's. ____ ____

8. One spouse should feel free to interrupt the other when he or she is concentrating on something and is in the same room. ____ ____

9. It is OK to open your spouse's *personal* mail without asking permission.

10. One should feel free to invite guests home without informing one's spouse. ____ ____

11. The main meal that the couple or family has together should be served at the same time every day. ____ ____

Communication
12. Some problems will disappear if you avoid arguing about them. ____ ____

13. In a relationship it is better to avoid conflicts than to engage in them. ____ ____

14. It is better to hide one's true feelings in order to avoid hurting your spouse. ____ ____

15. It is sometimes OK for one spouse to force the other to do things that he or she does not want to do. ____ ____

16. It is usually OK to argue in front of friends or in public places. ____ ____

The International View

Can you think of any other ideology or communication issues that would be important for discussing marriage in your country?

Divorce

Objective

to explore the criterion of *fault* in a just settlement following a divorce

Introduction

Our investigation crosses several realms. We will become aware of gender differences in marital issues. No other issue divides the sexes in a classroom setting as clearly as the issue of property rights tends to. The reason may be that it hits people where, supposedly, it hurts most—in the wallet. In addition to looking at this issue in relation to psychology (the major topic of this chapter), we will examine it in studying philosophy (chap. 4) and law (chap. 5).

Alimony is the money that one spouse pays the other as a result of divorce. Generally it goes from the husband to the wife. It can be a settlement (one-time large sum) or a monthly allowance that will continue until the recipient remarries. It does not include money for *child support*—that is a separate item, referring to payments for food, clothing, and other expenses that go along with raising children. Alimony is more like a living allowance. In some states it doesn't matter who is at fault in causing the divorce; in others, it does matter.

Introductory Question (Discuss)

To your knowledge, in your country does it matter who is at fault when determining how much money to award in alimony?

Vocabulary Gloss

amicably   =   in a friendly manner
virtually   =   practically, approximately

Procedure

Should *fault* be a factor in determining the amount of alimony? We will consider each of the following cases (a, b, c) one at a time. In small groups you will come up with a common decision on how much, if anything, should be paid, *per year.* The teacher will write the decision of each group on the chalkboard for each case as it is finished. You will have an opportunity to discuss the virtues and justice of the different groups' responses.

a.   Bob and Betty Jones are divorcing *amicably** after ten years. He makes $100,000. She is a housewife. There are no children. No one is at fault.

b.   John and Jane Jones (twins of Bob and Betty!) are divorcing after ten years but inamicably. John has been unfaithful. The couple make the same money as Bob and Betty, and *virtually** everything else is the same. Should John pay more than Bob in alimony? How much should he pay?

c.   Anthony and Amanda Jones (actually, there were two sets of triplets, not twins!) are divorcing after ten years, inamicably. Amanda has been unfaithful. Anthony makes the same money as his brothers, and everything else is virtually the same. How much should Anthony pay?

The International View

How and to what extent is divorce in your country different from divorce in the United States?

Rationality (Sunk Costs)

Objectives

> to practice dealing with a concept (rationality) that will play a role in many college courses

> to examine a concept from different points of view—economic, psychological, philosophical

Vocabulary Gloss

freak	=	(slang) person obsessed with something
cohesive	=	sticking together
vacillating	=	changing one's mind often
start from scratch	=	start from zero

Introduction

We would all agree that decision making demands rational choice, but *what is rational* is a subject of much debate, as we shall see as you discuss sunk costs. In fact, *rationality* crosses numerous disciplines and is taught as a course in both psychology and philosophy.

Sunk costs are an investment already made. They can be money, time, emotion, or even lives. Paying attention to these *(honoring sunk costs)* is considered irrational by economists because decisions should be based only on future considerations. But maybe economists don't know as much as they think they do.

For instance *(we will talk about this in class as part of our introduction to the subject)*, do you ever go to a restaurant, eat until you are full, then keep eating *because you paid a lot for it?* You don't want it, but you keep eating it anyway? Many of us have had this experience, and by continuing to eat we are *honoring a sunk cost;* we are acting irrationally, according to the economists. Whether you eat more or stop eating has no effect on the money *you have already spent.* That money is gone. So why keep eating?

Another example: Your country is building a big, expensive dam. The government has sunk millions of dollars into it. Then it becomes clear that the money made from the electricity the dam produces (that is the only purpose of the dam) will be less than the money needed to complete the dam. Should the project be abandoned? If the building continues, more money is being spent in order to lose money, which is completely irrational. Yet countries do this all the time. And supposedly smart people say foolish things.

To terminate a project in which $1.1 billion has been
invested represents an unconscionable mishandling of
taxpayers' dollars.

—Senator Denton, 4 Nov., 1981

Completing Tennessee-Tombigbee [Waterway Project] is not
a waste of taxpayer dollars. Terminating the project at
this late stage of development would, however, represent
a serious waste of funds already invested.

—Senator Sasser, 4 Nov., 1981

"But, Senator Sasser" (you want to say), "not terminating the project means wasting the funds already invested *and* funds that are not yet wasted but will be. Of course, you will have a beautiful dam, but it will be like a hole in your pocket from which our tax dollars will continually flow, like the water the dam is supposed to hold back."

Third example: You are an astronomy *freak.*° Your friend Hank, the artistic director of *Sky and Telescope* magazine, calls and tells you that tomorrow there will be an eclipse of the sun in Bora Bora, and there won't be another for a hundred years. Unfortunately, you have bought an unrefundable plane ticket to New York to go to a museum. You would much rather watch the eclipse of the sun, and you won't be able to see it on the plane, but you choose to go to New York *because you already paid for the ticket.*

This is *honoring a sunk cost.* Whether you go to New York or not, that money is spent, and it should not be a factor in your decision making—if you want to be rational.

But these examples may not be as clear and simple as they seem. There may be other influences in the decision-making process that are not irrational. For instance, in the dam example, if the politicians were thinking of the additional jobs that would be created, they would be thinking of the future and not honoring sunk costs.

And if you go to New York instead of watching the eclipse because you are worried about losing face with your friends, who would say that you wasted your money, then your decision may not be irrational since losing face is a future consideration.

Similarly, many people defended continuing the Vietnam War because to stop it would have meant that there was no good reason for thousands of deaths that had already occurred. These defenders of the war were honoring a sunk cost. But there were others who wanted to continue the war in order to show the world that we would not abandon other countries when situations became difficult. This second group of people were not making an irrational decision; they were not honoring a sunk cost but thinking of future considerations.

We all like to see our lives as *cohesive.** We don't like to cut ourselves off from our past. Even if our past decisions are foolish ones, we see them as part of us, and it is frightening to abandon them because we then face serious questions of identity. The person who chooses to watch the eclipse may be seen by his friends as disordered, unstable, *vacillating,** and unpredictable. These are not positive characteristics, and we don't like to be perceived in these ways.

So in the final analysis, the economists' notion of rationality may not be the only one. Couldn't we say, for example, that what is rational is what most of the people do most of the time, no matter what that is? At any rate, probably everyone would agree that in order to be rational we must not be contradictory. You should bear this last point in mind as you do the *sunk cost* experiments.

Procedure

Students will be assigned to the experiments in pairs. Each of you will ask five people *(preferably native speakers)* your *sunk cost* question and record their answers. Then you will meet or use the telephone to exchange data. In class, one of you will present the experiment to the class. Your teacher will give each student a photocopy of the *Peer Feedback Sheet* that appears in chapter 7, and the class will rate your presentation. You will answer any questions the class has about the experiment. Then students will defend their own opinions and discuss the issue. The presenters should actively participate in the discussion, especially from the point of view of sunk cost. Finally, you will ask for a show of hands for *yes* or *no*. The second student will write on the chalkboard (1) the results of original experiment, (2) the results of the ten people asked, and (3) the class's results.

When you present the case to the five people and ask their opinions, try to do as much of it as possible without reading from your books. You don't need to memorize the situation, just present it accurately. Above all, do not let the interviewee read the experiment! This task is designed to make you speak and explain clearly; it is not a reading task for someone else.

Experiment 1

You and your best friend Bob are big football fans, and you spent $100 each for two tickets for the last game of the season, between your favorite team, the Boston Patriots, and the New York Jets. On the morning of the game, as you eat breakfast, you watch a snowstorm develop, and the temperature drops to 15 degees Fahrenheit (minus 9 degrees Celsius). Because of new laws against re-selling of tickets, you cannot sell the ticket, and it is too late to return it. You and your friend both agree that you would find it more enjoyable to watch the game on TV than to spend several hours in the cold and the snow. Will you go to the game or stay home?

Use the following chart to record your results.

Results of 10 People Asked	*Number*	*Percent*
Go to the game	_____	_____%
Stay home	_____	_____%

Class Results	*Number*	*Percent*
	_____	_____%
	_____	_____%

Experiment 2

A few months ago you bought a $100 ticket for a weekend ski trip to Vermont. Several weeks later you bought a $50 ticket for a weekend ski trip to New Hampshire. You think that you will enjoy the New Hampshire ski trip more than the Vermont ski trip. As you put your just-purchased ticket in your wallet, you notice that the Vermont ski trip and the New Hampshire ski trip are both for the weekend that starts tomorrow! It's too late to sell either ticket, and you cannot return either one. You must use one ticket and not the other. Which ski trip will you go on? Why?

The results obtained when this experiment originally was conducted are presented first, followed by a blank chart for you to use in recording your own results.

Which ski trip will you go on?

Experiments 2, 3, and 4 were adapted from material created by Hal Arkes and Catherine Blumer in "The Psychology of Sunk Costs," *Organizational Behavior and Human Decision Processes* 35 (1985).

Original Experiment Results	Number	Percent
$100 ski trip to Vermont	66	54%
$50 ski trip to New Hampshire	56	46%

Results of 10 People Asked	Number	Percent
	____	____%
	____	____%

Class Results	Number	Percent
	____	____%
	____	____%

Experiment 3

(Students doing this experiment should also read experiment 4.) As the president of Rational Airlines, you have invested 10 million dollars of the company's money in a research project. The purpose was to build a warplane that would not be detected by conventional radar—in other words, a radar-blank plane. When the project is 90% completed, another company begins selling a very similar plane that cannot be detected by radar. As far as you can tell, the major differences between your plane and theirs are that their plane is much faster and costs far less to operate than the plane your company is building. The question is, should you invest the last 10% of the research funds to build the radar-blank plane, or should you abandon the project?

The results obtained when this experiment originally was conducted are presented first, followed by a blank chart for you to use in recording your own results.

Original Experiment Results	Number	Percent
Yes	82	85%
No	14	15%

Results of 10 People Asked	Number	Percent
Yes	____	____%
No	____	____%

Class Results	Number	Percent
Yes	____	____%
No	____	____%

Experiment 4

(Students doing this experiment should also read experiment 3.) As president of
Trans-Rational Airlines, you have received a suggestion from one of your employees. The suggestion is to use the last 10 million dollars of your research
funds to develop a plane that would not be detected by conventional radar, in
other words, a radar-blank plane. However, another firm has just begun marketing a plane that cannot be detected by radar. Also, it is apparent that their plane
is much faster and far more economical than the plane your company could
build. The question is, should you invest the last 10 million dollars of your research funds to build the radar-blank plane proposed by your employee? (*Note:*
Here, you are *starting from scratch,*° and the 10 million is the total sum needed
to produce the plane.)

The results obtained when this experiment originally was conducted are presented first, followed by a blank chart for you to use in recording your own results.

Original Experiment Results	*Number*	*Percent*
Yes	20	17%
No	100	83%

Results of 10 People Asked	*Number*	*Percent*
Yes	_____	_____%
No	_____	_____%

Class Results	*Number*	*Percent*
Yes	_____	_____%
No	_____	_____%

Experiment 5

You have decided to see a play. The price is $10 per ticket. Standing in the ticket
line, you discover that you have lost a $10 bill. Would you still pay $10 for the
play? (*Note:* You have enough money to do so.)

The results obtained when this experiment originally was conducted are presented first, followed by a blank chart for you to use in recording your own results.

Experiments 5 and 6 are adapted with permission from Amos Tversky and Daniel Kahneman, "The
Framing of Decisions and the Psychology of Choice," *Science* 211 (January 30, 1981). Copyright 1981
American Association for the Advancement of Science.

Original Experiment Results	Number	Percent
Yes	322	88%
No	42	12%

Results of 10 People Asked	Number	Percent
Yes	____	____%
No	____	____%

Class Results	Number	Percent
Yes	____	____%
No	____	____%

Experiment 6

You have bought a ticket to a play for $10. The doors open, and everybody starts to enter the theater. You reach into your pocket for the ticket you know you put there, and you can't find it. You search but can't find it anywhere. You have lost the ticket. The seat was not marked, and it is hopeless to think that you will find it. But there are still tickets on sale. Would you pay $10 for another ticket? (You have enough money to do so.)

The results obtained when this experiment originally was conducted are presented first, followed by a blank chart for you to use in recording your own results.

Original Experiment Results	Number	Percent
Yes	184	46%
No	216	54%

Results of 10 People Asked	Number	Percent
Yes	____	____%
No	____	____%

Class Results	Number	Percent
Yes	____	____%
No	____	____%

The International View

Do large numbers of people in your country do things that you or others consider irrational?

Can you recall any incident in your life or any governmental decision that illustrates the *sunk cost* phenomenon?

Synergy (Lost at Sea)

Objectives

   to introduce the concept of synergy

   to understand group dynamics

   to understand that you can learn from your colleagues, as opposed to
      having knowledge poured into your heads by a teacher

   to practice using *Conversation Cues* for *Changing Your Mind, Asking for
      Repetition,* and *Interruption*

Introduction

This is an exercise in group decision making. More specifically, it is an exercise
in synergy. Synergy is the concept that "two heads are better than one." In other
words, when considering an issue, a group of people should be able to make a
better decision than any individual in the group. We will test this concept.

   Native speakers usually experience synergy in group discussion. Students
who are learning another language often do not achieve synergy. There are two
major reasons for this. One is that students who do very well individually may be
shy and will not try to persuade the others of their opinions. The other is that
some students who do not do well individually may love to talk and may be very
forceful. Thus you should be sure to get all of your group members to share the
reasons for their choices and avoid letting any one student dominate your discussion.

Vocabulary Gloss

yacht	=	luxurious boat
life raft	=	small emergency boat that you inflate with air
crew	=	people who work on a boat
oars	=	long, wooden instruments used to move a boat or raft
sextant	=	navigational device for use with stars
seat cushion	=	comfortable thing to sit on, like on an airplane
shark repellent	=	liquid that should make sharks go away
20 square feet	=	5 feet high by 4 feet long
opaque	=	blocking the passage of light; can't be seen through
fishing kit	=	little box with the essentials for fishing

Lost at Sea

As a consequence of a fire of unknown origin, your *yacht** is slowly sinking in the South Pacific. Your location is unclear because the fire destroyed much of the navigational equipment. Your best estimate is that you're approximately 1,000 miles southwest of the nearest land.

Below is a list of 15 items that are undamaged after the fire. In addition to these articles, you have a rubber *life raft** with *oars** that is large enough to carry yourself and the four *crew** members and all of the items listed below. Along with these, you have in your collective pockets one package of cigarettes, several books of matches, and 5 one-dollar bills.

Part 1

Procedure

You will rank the 15 items in terms of their importance to your survival. Place the number *1* by the most important item, the number *2* by the second most important, and so on through number *15*, the least important. Ask the class if you don't understand any of the items.

_____ *sextant**
_____ shaving mirror
_____ five-gallon can of water

_____   mosquito netting
_____   one case (24 cans) emergency food
_____   maps of the Pacific Ocean
_____   *seat cushion*° (flotation device)
_____   two-gallon can of oil-gas mixture
_____   one "Walkman" radio
_____   *shark repellent*°
_____   20 *square feet*° of *opaque*° plastic
_____   one quart of strong rum, 80% alcohol (that is, 160 proof)
_____   15 feet of nylon rope
_____   two boxes of chocolate bars
_____   *fishing kit*°

Part 2

Procedure

You will be working with the *Individual/Consensus* ranking sheet that follows.

1. Copy your own ranking for each item into the column that says "Repeat Individual."

2. Now you will work in groups of three or four. Discuss your *individual* rankings in whatever way you think best and come up with a consensus about a group ranking. If you *cannot* get a majority, say 2 to 1, then do not force the minority member to accept your solution: instead, you must try to convince him or her that your decision is best. You must find a solution that *everyone* can accept, even though perhaps no one person thinks that it is best. You should consider differences of opinion as a help rather than a hindrance in achieving your goal. Find out why the other person chose what he or she did. One way to start is to say, "OK, what did you put for number one?" At some point, you could work from the bottom (15) up. Write the ranking of the group in the column marked "Group Consensus."

3. The teacher will read you the *best ranking*, as decided by officers of the U. S. Merchant Marines. You may not agree with the rationale for these choices, but we must accept it.

4. Write the "correct" ranking in the appropriate column.

5. Find the difference between your individual ranking and the "correct" ranking, and put that on the same line as your own individual ranking, to the right of your ranking. It doesn't matter if the difference is a positive (+) or negative (-) number. Just use the number; ignore any minus (-) sign.

6. Now find the difference between the group consensus and the correct ranking. Put this number on the same line as the group consensus ranking. Again, it doesn't matter if it is a positive or a negative number. Just use the number.

7. Total the scores for *Individual* and *Group.*

(Hypothetical Example)

Correct	*Repeat Individual*	*Group Consensus*
3	1 (2)	7 (4)

You chose 1. Therefore, your score is 2 [the difference between 3 and 1]. The group chose 7. The group score is 4 [the difference between 3 and 7]. Note that the best score is the lowest. A perfect score would be zero.

Correct	*Repeat Individual*	*Group Consensus*	
_____	_____	_____	sextant
_____	_____	_____	shaving mirror
_____	_____	_____	five-gallon can of water
_____	_____	_____	mosquito netting
_____	_____	_____	one case (24 cans) emergency food
_____	_____	_____	maps of the Pacific Ocean
_____	_____	_____	seat cushion (flotation device)
_____	_____	_____	two-gallon can of oil-gas mixture
_____	_____	_____	one "Walkman" radio
_____	_____	_____	shark repellent
_____	_____	_____	20 square feet of opaque plastic
_____	_____	_____	one quart of strong rum, 80% alcohol (that is, 160 proof)
_____	_____	_____	15 feet of nylon rope
_____	_____	_____	two boxes of chocolate bars
_____	_____	_____	fishing kit
	_____	_____	*(Total)*

Synergy Analysis

The teacher will quickly record individual scores (without names) and the group scores. He or she will turn over this data to one student who will be responsible for filling in the following tables and reporting the results to the class the next day.

Before Group Discussion

Group Number	Average Individual Score in the Group	Most Accurate Individual Score in the Group
(Example)	55	45
1		
2		
3		
4		

	Average Individual Score for All Groups	Most Accurate Individual Score Averaged across All Groups
	____	____

After Group Discussion

Group Number	Score for Group Consensus	Gain/Loss over Average Individual	Gain/Loss over Most Accurate Individual	Synergy* (yes/no)
(Example)	40	+15**	+5	Yes
1				
2				
3				
4				
Average				

Synergy will be defined as a consensus score lower than the lowest individual score in the group.

**+15 means that this consensus score was 15 better than the individual score, even though it was 15 lower. Remember, the lower the score, the better it is. A minus (-) would indicate that the consensus score was worse, that is, a larger number.

Conclusion

We will discuss why some groups achieved synergy and others did not. We will also discuss what behaviors helped or hindered the consensus-seeking process.

Conversation Cues

(Keep your book open to this page or write the cues on a separate piece of paper. Put a check mark next to a cue each time you use it.)

Changing Your Mind

On second thought, . . .

Asking for Repetition

I didn't catch that. Could you repeat that?

Interruption

I'd like to jump in.

Can I jump in?

Let me jump in here.

Can I just say that . . .

Can I get my two cents in?

I'd like to get my two cents in, if you don't mind.

The International View

Can you think of any incidents in your personal experience where "two heads have been better than one"? Or were you ever involved in an incident where synergy was counterproductive—where "two heads were worse than one"?

4

Philosophy
(Distributive Justice)

The Candy Bar Dilemma

Objectives

to develop debating skills

to create an argument

to listen to and counter other arguments

to write from a strong thesis

to understand and employ the principle of *charity* in persuasive writing
and oral argument

Introduction

This apparently simple exercise is a microcosm of issues in distributive justice, a
subject that has become increasingly popular in philosophy. Distributive justice
examines fairness in holdings—how do we justify having those things we have?
This subject is different from *criminal justice*, which we will take up in chapter
5, *Law*.

But first, what comes to your mind when you think about the term *distributive justice*? Is this an issue that has special significance in your country?

Vocabulary Gloss

propensity	=	natural tendency
break out in zits	=	to develop pimples (little spots, generally on the face and sometimes associated with eating sweets)
arbiter	=	judge

The Candy Bar Dilemma

On the table is one candy bar. Three teenagers want it. Andrew has a *propensity** to *break out in zits.** Betty is obese. Carol is normal in all respects, but she has just eaten three candy bars. You must distribute the candy bar justly. How will you do it?

On the table is a candy bar. Three teenagers want it.

Procedure

Part 1. How the Candy Bar Should Be Distributed Justly
Discuss the possibilities, as a class. Be sure to suggest all reasonable possibilities of distribution (you can divide it or give it wholly). Give reasons pro and con (for and against).

Part 2. Role Play
You will be divided into groups of four. Each of you will have a role as Andrew, Betty, Carol, or *arbiter.** The teacher will give the arbiter one candy bar. The arbiter will listen to arguments from the three "teenagers," who will say why they want it and why the others should not get it. The arbiter will award the entire (not divided) candy bar to the teenager who offers the best arguments. (The arbiter will also get a candy bar.)

Writing Assignment

Write your own opinion on Part 1: *How the Candy Bar Should Be Distributed Justly.* Your written opinion should be one-half page minimum, one page maximum.

You are writing a philosophical argument. In doing this, you must not only present your opinion but also show why the alternative solutions are not so good. And here you must pay attention to the principle of *charity.* As explained in chapter 2, the principle of charity in a philosophical argument means that you consider only the strongest arguments contrary to yours. If you can destroy the strongest opposing arguments, the weaker ones will automatically fall.

Thus when dealing with opposing arguments you will ignore, for example, the argument that "Andrew should get the whole candy bar because his name starts with the letter *A.*" There are stronger arguments for Andrew getting it all.

The International View

Are there problems of distributive justice in your country (e.g., land distribution or redistribution of state-owned enterprises)?

The Race

Objectives

analytic thinking

creativity in argument

to practice using *Conversation Cues* for *Strong Disagreement*

Introduction

In any course you may take, you will have to establish criteria for your decisions. But are criteria philosophically rigid, fixed in stone?

Vocabulary Gloss

track	=	sport of running various distances, jumping, and so forth
make the team	=	meet the criteria for being on the team
trip	=	to make someone fall by interfering with leg motion
sluggish	=	tired and slow-moving, having no energy

Part 1

The high school *track* * team is going to hold a race. The race will determine who is to *make the team.* * Anyone who runs the 100 meter race in 12 seconds or under is on the team. Jesse, Harry, Carlos, and Ben fail to meet the criterion, but each of them demands a second chance.

Consider the reasons that each of them gives and decide whether that runner's claim is valid, that is, *if he should be given a second chance.* Assume that all the stories are true and that there is room for more on the track team.

a. *Jesse* says that Fred *tripped* * him. This is clear from the videotape. It also looks like Fred tripped him deliberately. (Should Fred be disqualified?)

Jesse says that Fred tripped him.

b. *Harry* says that the other guys ate his breakfast so that he would not have enough energy to run fast. It is true that the other guys don't like him much and also true that Harry runs better after a good breakfast. He also ran out of vitamins that day, and we know that they always make him run faster.

c. *Carlos* says he felt very *sluggish*° that day and was probably fighting off a cold. His father was a star runner, as was his grandfather. Carlos wants more than anything to make his father proud of him and to follow in his father's footsteps. He says his family would die of disappointment if he didn't make the team.

d. *Ben* says he had a headache on the day of the race. He has always been in trouble with the law. When he was on the junior high track team last year he managed to stay out of trouble for the first time in his life. He is afraid that if he doesn't make the team he will start stealing or doing drugs again.

Procedure

1. The class as a whole will briefly discuss each case.

2. You will break into small groups and try to reach a consensus. Everyone must state his or her opinion on each case.

3. You will report to the class as a whole your group's consensus.

Part 2
You have tried but failed to make the track team. Prepare a reason for getting a second chance. You will be divided into small groups again, with different people, and one student will be appointed as mediator. Only one student in each group will be given a second chance—the one with the most convincing and believable argument. Begin clockwise from the mediator, presenting your reason(s) for a second chance. The other students should criticize these reasons. Feel free to interrupt at any time.

Conversation Cues

(Keep your book open to this page or write the cues on a separate piece of paper. Put a check mark next to a cue each time you use it.)

Strong Disagreement

Are you kidding?

You must be joking!

Come off it!

You can't be serious.

Surely, you jest.

Get real!

No way!

Come on!

Notes

"Surely, you jest" is an old, formal, and humorous expression. "Jest" means "joke."

Writing Assignment: Criteria for Accepting Claims for a Second Chance

Which claims, if any, did you accept? Why not accept all the claims? Why some and not others? What criteria underlie your choice?

You may write about Jesse, Ben, Carlos, and Harry; or you may write about the group experience in Part 2. Your paper should be approximately one page long.

The International View

In your country, are criteria for making teams or for getting into schools rigidly applied? Or are they flexible? Do individual circumstances mean a lot in bending criteria? Think of a specific example.

Mrs. Kerr and Ms. Pink

Objectives

to explore our beliefs about the right of transference of property

(secondarily) to consider animal rights

Introduction

This scenario is based on a true event that took place in upper New York State some years ago. The basic principles that you will discuss relate not only to philosophy but to *law*.

Vocabulary Gloss

widow	=	woman whose husband has died
poodle	=	pretty little dog with thick, curly hair
show . . . off	=	to display with pride
dazzling	=	brilliantly shining, very impressive
mink	=	animal whose fur is used for very expensive coats
bag lady	=	homeless woman who carries all her belongings in shopping bags
lavish	=	spend large sums of money carelessly

Procedure

Read the two parts carefully. In small groups, discuss Ms. Pink's contentions, which appear in Part 1. You will be assigned for homework a role for Part 2. See the "Procedure" section that follows Part 2 for further instructions.

Mrs. Kerr and Ms. Pink

Part 1

A rich old *widow,** Mrs. Kerr, lives at 300 Central Park West in New York City. She has a *poodle,** which she claims is her only friend in the world. Her greatest (and only) joy in life is taking the poodle for a walk in the park every morning and *showing* him *off.** The poodle is a *dazzling** sight and not an uncommon one in New York City. He has a *mink** jacket worth $3,000, a diamond necklace worth $50,000, a jeweled crown worth $20,000, and diamond earrings worth another $20,000.

Ms. Pink, a communist *bag lady,** takes a walk in Central Park every day at the same time Mrs. Kerr does. Ms. Pink says it is unjust that Mrs. Kerr *lavish** all that wealth on an animal. She says (1) that the jewelry should be taken away by the state and given to needy, starving people. She also says (2) that a law should be passed making it illegal to spend more than $1,000 on a pet.

What do you think of Ms. Pink's two contentions?

Ms. Pink says it is unjust that Mrs. Kerr lavish all that wealth on an animal.

Part 2

Mrs. Kerr dies, leaving all her money to her poodle until the animal dies, at which time it will all go to charity. And how ironic it is that, after a long search by lawyers, it turns out that Mrs. Kerr's closest relative is . . . Ms. Pink!—her long lost twin sister, separated from her shortly after birth by a shipwreck.

Ms. Pink contests Mrs. Kerr's will in court. It seems that Mrs. Kerr also instructed in her will that her big summerhouse, located on a large estate in the mountains of upstate New York, be burned down with everything in it. She has made a generous gift to the fire department to supervise the burning.

The property on which the estate is located will be donated to charity.

Is it just that the poodle get the money?

Is it just that the house be burned down?

Procedure for Role Play

Half of you will be instructed to prepare the role of Mrs. Kerr, and the other half, Ms. Pink. Mrs. Kerr is on her deathbed and has just written her will, assigning all of her property to her poodle. Ms. Pink has just been made aware that she is the only living relative of Mrs. Kerr. You must invent all the details of your lives: where you have lived, your life history, how you were separated, and so forth. Practice speaking to yourself, going over all the facets of your (new) life.

In class you will be divided into groups of three: Mrs. Kerr, Ms. Pink, and an arbiter. The arbiter judges the case objectively (forgetting the life history that he or she has prepared for Mrs. Kerr or Ms. Pink), based entirely on the arguments given by the players. When all the groups are finished, each arbiter will tell the class why he or she chose to validate or invalidate the will.

The International View

Do animals have rights in your country? Or can people treat them any way they want? (For example, in the United States there are laws against abusing a pet, and some groups are trying to outlaw laboratory experiments on animals, saying that the practice is cruel.)

Finders, Keepers

Objective

to reflect on the basic philosophical issue of property rights and to articulate your thoughts

Introduction

In any introductory philosophy course you will face the issue of property rights. By doing this exercise, you will feel comfortable dealing with the issue. You will understand what the problems are, and you will be able to articulate your own view. Your views will be changed and enriched by hearing the ideas of your classmates. At the same time, you will have fun in the discussion.

Along the way, you will deal with philosopher John Locke's famous *proviso* that you can do what you want with property as long as there be "enough and as good left in common for others."

You should be stimulated to think about how we come to *own* anything.

Introductory Question

For homework, in preparation for class, think about this: Do parents own their children? We will start the next class with a brief debate on this topic. You will also read the "Finders, Keepers" scenario for homework, and we will discuss the following question in small groups: *Is it just that Stuart retain sole possession of all the goods?*

Also, for homework, think of five items that you would add to the list of items found by Stuart.

Procedure

In class, your small group is the class that has been shipwrecked. Decide how the goods are to be distributed. One of you will volunteer for or will be assigned the role of Stuart. When you have finished, each group will tell the class what distribution it actually made and how the distribution was decided on.

Vocabulary Gloss

shipwrecked	=	having one's ship sunk
on the spur of the moment	=	deciding instantly
can't help but X	=	can't avoid doing X
boom boxes	=	big, loud, portable radios
scout	=	look around
mourn	=	feel sad at the death or loss of

Finders, Keepers

You, the students of this class, have been *shipwrecked.** Fortunately, you all survived, swimming to the shores of the uninhabited tropical island of Nadur with just the shirts on your backs. Unfortunately, no one knows where you are. No one even knows that you all had left, *on the spur of the moment,** for a cruise on one student's boat.

Although you'd rather be home again, you *can't help but** find the island a paradise. The climate is delightfully warm, day and night. There are no dangerous animals to contend with. Fruit of all kinds grows plentifully on trees. Vegetables grow wild.

You miss, however, your *boom boxes** and all the comforts of home. All of your belongings went down with the ship. Now, on the morning after the shipwreck, you gather together on the beach and decide to *scout** about the small island. Only one of your classmates is missing—Stuart. You *mourn** him, but not too much—nobody cared a great deal for him anyway. But as it turns out,

Stuart is not dead—he is just an early riser, and he has already gone off to scout the island. When you encounter the big, strong Stuart an hour later, he is standing proudly on a bunch of boxes he has retrieved, with his own labor, from the edge of the sea. He has just concluded an inventory. These boxes, which are *not* from your ship, contain the following items.

3 bottles of Dom Perignon champagne

1 volleyball net and ball

2 mosquito nets

3 fishing poles

1 bottle of quinine

1 standard first aid kit

1 gun with ammunition

3 plastic containers of sunscreen

1 thousand-dollar bill

(Write in five more items your group agrees on.)

_____

_____

_____

_____

_____

You approach Stuart with broad smiles that turn to frowns as Stuart says, "Finders, keepers!"

A careful search of the island turns up nothing more. But in fact, at present you do not need any of the items Stuart has assembled.

The International View

Does your country have a strong tradition of private property? Are there things that cannot be owned privately but must belong to all the people?

Joe, His Bread, the Lifeboat

Objectives

to examine how deeply we believe in property rights

to develop criteria for a just distribution of goods

Introduction

Lifeboat scenarios are often used to push our beliefs to an extreme. When you make your own arguments, in any subject, you may want to use a similar scenario to test some principle. For a principle or a belief to be valid, it must apply in all cases. Therefore, you create an extreme situation. If the principle is valid here, it should be valid in all cases. The scenario that we discuss here may have a happy ending.

Vocabulary Gloss

drifting   =   moving on a current of water, without power
rowing   =   using oars to move a boat

Procedure

In small groups you will answer the questions that are part of the scenario that follows.

Ten men are in a lifeboat at sea. They have been *drifting** for five days and have consumed, they think, all of their food. Everyone is very hungry, because they have been *rowing** for five days in hope of reaching land. At first they had a reasonable expectation of success. Now, however, only Arnold has strength enough to row.

Suddenly, Joe reaches into his bag and produces a loaf of bread that his wife had baked to help him in case of just such an emergency. He smiles and thanks his wife for her prudent, wise, and lifesaving forethought.

1. Does Joe have a right to eat the loaf by himself, as he would like to do?

2. Should he share it with all the others, equally?

3. Some of the men are much bigger than the others and need more to survive. Should they get more?

4. Arnold thinks he should get it all. Does he have a good case for his suggestion?

5. Since Arnold is the only one still strong enough to row, he is also capable of taking the loaf from Joe by force and eating it all. If the other men don't agree with Arnold's suggestion, does he have a right to take the loaf?

The International View

Is there ever starvation in your country, or are the hungry always taken care of by the government or by family or relatives?

Sam and the Posse

Objective

to test our beliefs about property rights

Introduction

Most of us believe that what is ours is ours—in other words, that we have rights over our property. If I leave my hat in your car it does not become yours, right? I can demand that you give it back, right? We will test these assumptions. (This scenario is similar to one devised by philosopher Immanuel Kant and may prepare you for discussion aspects of Kant's philosophy, as well as property rights.)

Procedure

In small groups, discuss the questions that follow the scenario about Sam. When you finish, the teacher will elicit a quick summary of responses to the situation.

Vocabulary Gloss

slain	=	(past participle of *slay*) killed
in cold blood	=	mercilessly, with no remorse
ammunition	=	bullets (pieces of lead that come out of a gun when it is shot)
homicidal	=	having tendency to kill
posse	=	group of community members loosely organized by local law enforcement officials to hunt down a criminal

Sam is a killer and is being hunted by the sons of the man he has just *slain** in *cold blood.** He has a gun but no *ammunition.** He comes to your house and demands the box of ammunition he left there last week. Of course, you didn't know at that time what a *homicidal** maniac he was. The sounds of the *posse** can be heard outside. Sam is sure that they will shoot him dead. Will you give him his box of ammunition? Exactly what will you do? What does your decision say about your view of property rights?

The International View

Who has the right to own a gun in your country? Everyone? In your opinion, should this right be extended to more people or restricted to fewer?

5

Law

Crime and Punishment

Objectives

to understand the U. S. judicial system and how it differs from others

to understand the complexity and difficulty of applying concepts to real events

Introduction

In any course you take, you will have to define terms. But that definition must work in real situations. In this unit we will see that "murder" depends on the concept of "intention." But though we use this word with no problem, it is not as simple as it appears.

Before going any further, we need to understand more fully the U. S. judicial system. The system is called "common law" and is similar to England's system. It differs in some respects from European and other judicial systems. Whenever you notice a difference, mention it. The comparison will be interesting and useful.

In American law, we draw an objective line between *wrongdoing* (the crime) and *attribution* (excuses based on particular circumstances). If you are insane, the wrongdoing cannot be attributed to you. If you are pregnant and starving when you steal, you are less guilty.

In European law, attribution tends to be built into the crime. So "killing by insanity" is a separate kind of crime.

In criminal justice, problems arise because language is often ambiguous. For example, the crime of murder depends on the notion of *intention*. In order for a crime to be classified as a murder, there must be *clear intention*. But without a confession, we can only guess at a person's intention. This raises serious problems. Think about the following questions and scenarios, then write your opinions underneath the scenarios (unless your teacher asks you to write them on a separate sheet of paper and hand them in). Be prepared to discuss your opinions in class.

Scenarios 4 and 8 are similar to events in the films *Mortal Thoughts* and *Reversal of Fortune.* These films raise interesting questions about the problematic nature of *intention,* which is necessary for a crime to be murder. The class may want to see these films.

Vocabulary Gloss

diabetic	=	person having disease of diabetes (high blood sugar)
insulin	=	medication taken by diabetics
cyanide	=	poison
syringe	=	hypodermic needle
shot	=	injection
tumor	=	an abnormal mass of tissue growth
crib	=	baby's enclosed bed
bum	=	lazy, unsuccessful person who doesn't work
arsenic	=	poison
go off	=	explode
remorse	=	sorrow or guilt over past wrongdoing
dismantles	=	takes apart
hijacked	=	forcibly took control of vehicle
rapist	=	person who rapes (forces sexual intercourse)
suffocates	=	dies from lack of air
at the end of her rope	=	psychologically unable to continue in the situation
coroner	=	doctor who determines cause of death
surgeon	=	doctor who operates
delirious	=	mentally disturbed, extremely confused
strangles	=	kills by squeezing throat and stopping breathing

Procedure

Read these at home and decide on your responses. Discussion will be done as a class, or in small groups, or a mixture of both. In all cases, one student will read the scenario and the teacher will call on students to give their opinions, which will be either read or spoken (preferably the latter). Questions about the vocabulary will be taken right after the reading. Try to reach a consensus. When you have finished, the teacher will ask each group to tell the class its consensus opinion of all, or of selected, scenarios.

If you recall any similar scenarios, make sure to share them with the class.

1. *George* plans to kill his wife, who is a *diabetic.* He plans to inject her with poison. Alan learns of this and substitutes *insulin* in the bottle of *cyanide.* George fills up the *syringe* and gives her a good-bye *shot.* She survives. Then Alan tells the police.

Is George guilty of a crime? If so, what is it? What could George say in his defense? What role does *intention* play here?

2. A *man* goes to the top of a ten-story tower in Texas with a rifle and starts firing at a crowd of people from a distance of about 100 meters. Two people die. Is this murder?

3. A *man* with a brain *tumor*° opens a window on the third floor of his house, then walks to his son's *crib*,° picks him up, and throws him out the window. Everyone says that he loved his son. Is this murder?

4. *Roseann* plans to kill her husband, an unfaithful *bum*.° She mixes enough *arsenic*° to kill an elephant into some sugar and asks her daughter to carry the sugar bowl upstairs to the bum, who is screaming for his sugar. She trips on the stairs, and Fido, their dog, licks the "sugar" and falls over dead. The clever daughter sweeps up the mess, throws it away along with Fido, puts real sugar in the bowl, and delivers it to her dad. Has Roseann committed a crime? Did she have the *intention* to kill?

5. *Ed,* a terrorist, plants a time bomb in the Park Street station, set to *go off*° at rush hour. He goes home, turns on the news, and is suddenly struck with *remorse*.° He rushes back to the station to turn off the bomb but arrives a half hour late. Fortunately, the bomb was defective and did not go off. He takes it back home and *dismantles*° it. Has Ed committed a crime? How does intention figure into it?

6. *Ed's* twin sister *Edwina* is a stewardess on an airplane that has been *hijacked*° by the terrible and infamous terrorist Patty Hearts. She orders the captain to change course and fly over Cuba. Expecting that Patty might use a parachute, Edwina cuts it with a knife. The terrorist has not harmed anyone. Patty jumps out with the defective chute and dies. Is Edwina guilty of murder? Of anything?

7. A *rapist*° places his hand over his victim's mouth, simply to keep her from calling for help. She *suffocates*° and dies. Is this murder?

8. *Roseann* is *at the end of her rope*.° She can't take another minute of living with Hannibal. While he is sleeping she stabs him through the heart with a steak knife. She leans over to kiss him good-bye and notices that his forehead is cold. The *coroner*° reports that Hannibal died of a drug overdose four hours earlier. Is Roseann guilty of a crime?

Roseann can't stand another minute of living with Hannibal.

9. *Jules* and *Jim* are in love with the same woman. Independently, they decide
    that Paris (the city where they live) is not big enough for both of them. Then,
    suddenly, Jim has an attack of appendicitis. Unfortunately for him, Jules is a
    skilled *surgeon.** He plans to make a regrettable mistake at the local hospi-
    tal. Jim, almost *delirious** with pain, looks up from the surgery table at Jules'
    smiling face. He grabs Jules by the throat and *strangles** him to death. Who
    is guilty of what?

The International View

In your legal system, is the accused assumed to be innocent until proven guilty
or assumed guilty until proven innocent? Which of these legal assumptions do
you think is better?

   Is there capital punishment (the death penalty) for murder in your country?

Presentation

Two students will be chosen to present their views on capital punishment (one
for and one against). You will have a predetermined amount of time (e.g., three
minutes) to present your point of view. You will not read your views, but you
may use note cards to help you remember what you want to say. When the
presentation is done, the rest of the class may offer their views.

Humor in the Court

Objective

to understand and appreciate humor in English

Introduction

These dialogues are real, not fictional. As you will see, humor can arise in the most serious situations. Although law is a very serious matter and profession, it involves ordinary people, and not all lawyers and prosecutors are brilliant. (The dialogues are from *More Humor in the Court,* by Mary Louise Gilman [Vienna, VA: National Court Reporters' Association, 1984].)

Vocabulary Gloss

lumbar region   =   lower back
deceased   =   dead
pursuant to   =   following
scalp   =   skin on top of head
skin graft   =   attachment of skin from one part of the body to another
                    part or from one person to another
buttocks   =   part of body that you sit on
fracas   =   a noisy quarrel

Procedure

As you read these dialgoues, note the one or ones that you find most funny. In class you will be asked to read that one and tell why it is funny. Also, note any examples that you don't understand. In class, your fellow students will explain them.

1. *Q:* What is your brother-in-law's name?

    A: Borofkin.

    Q: What's his first name?

    A: I can't remember.

    Q: He's been your brother-in-law for years, and you can't remember his first name?

    A: No. I tell you I'm too excited. (Rising from the witness chair and pointing to Mr. Borofkin.) Nathan, for God's sake, tell them your first name!

2. *Q:* Did you ever stay all night with this man in New York?

   A: I refuse to answer that question.

   Q: Did you ever stay all night with this man in Chicago?

   A: I refuse to answer that question.

   Q: Did you ever stay all night with this man in Miami?

   A: No.

3. *Q:* Now, Mrs. Johnson, how was your first marriage terminated?

   A: By death.

   Q: And by whose death was it terminated?

4. *Q:* Doctor, did you say he was shot in the woods?

   A: No, I said he was shot in the *lumbar region.**

5. *Q:* What is your name?

   A: Ernestine McDowell.

   Q: And what is your marital status?

   A: Fair.

6. *Q:* Are you married?

   A: No, I'm divorced.

   Q: And what did your husband do before you divorced him?

   A: A lot of things I didn't know about.

7. *Q:* Do you know how far pregnant you are right now?

   A: I will be three months November 8th.

   Q: Apparently then, the date of conception was August 8th?

   A: Yes.

   Q: What were you and your husband doing at that time?

8. *Q:* Mrs. Smith, do you believe that you are emotionally unstable?

   A: I should be.

   Q: How many times have you committed suicide?

   A: Four times.

9. *Q:* Doctor, how many autopsies have you performed on dead people?

   A: All my autopsies have been performed on dead people.

10. *Q:* Were you acquainted with the *deceased?**

   A: Yes, sir.

   Q: Before or after he died?

11. *Q:* Officer, what led you to believe the defendant was under the influence [of alcohol]?

   A: Because he was *argumentary* and he couldn't *pronunciate* his words.

12. *Q:* What happened then?

   A: He told me, he says, "I have to kill you because you can identify me."

   Q: Did he kill you?

   A: No.

13. *Q:* Mrs. Jones, is your appearance this morning *pursuant to** a deposition notice which I sent to your attorney?

   A: No. This is how I dress when I go to work.

14. *Q:* Did he pick the dog up by the ears?

   A: No.

   Q: What was he doing with the dog's ears?

   A: Picking them up in the air.

   Q: Where was the dog at this time?

   A: Attached to the ears.

15. *Q:* And lastly, Gary, all your responses must be oral. OK? What school
           do you go to?

     A: Oral.

     Q: How old are you?

     A: Oral.

16. *Q:* What is your relationship with the plaintiff?

     A: She is my daughter.

     Q: Was she your daughter on February 13, 1979?

17. *Q:* Now, you have investigated other murders, have you not, where there
           was a victim?

18. *Q:* Did you tell your lawyer that your husband had offered you indigni-
           ties?

     A: He didn't offer me nothing; he just said I could have the furniture.

19. *Q:* So, after the anesthesia, when you came out of it, what did you
           observe with respect to your *scalp?**

     A: I didn't see my scalp the whole time I was in the hospital.

     Q: It was covered?

     A: Yes, bandaged.

     Q: Then, later on. . . what did you see?

     A: I had a *skin graft.** My whole *buttocks** and leg were removed and
           put on top of my head.

20. *Q:* Could you see him from where you were standing?

     A: I could see his head.

     Q: And where was his head?

     A: Just above his shoulders.

21. *Q:* Are you sexually active?

    A: No, I just lie there.

22. *Q:* Are you qualified to give a urine sample?

    A: Yes, I have been since early childhood.

23. *Q:* The truth of the matter is that you were not an unbiased, objective
        witness, isn't it. You too were shot in the *fracas?*＊

    A: No, sir. I was shot midway between the fracas and the navel.

24. *Q:* What is the meaning of sperm being present?

    A: It indicates intercourse.

    Q: Male sperm?

    A: That is the only kind I know.

25. *Q:* (showing man picture) That's you?

    A: Yes, sir.

    Q: And you were present when the picture was taken, right?

26. *Q:* Was that the same nose you broke as a child?

The International View

Can you recall any strange or funny court stories from your country?

The Case of Humbert Phillips

Objectives

>   to discover how points of law are taught in U. S. law schools

>   to discuss legal issues

>   persuasive argument

>   to uncover inconsistencies in others' arguments

Introduction

In U.S. law schools, points of law are illustrated and debated by means of humorous scenarios that usually are not realistic. Final exams are often in the form of analysis of cases such as this one, *The Case of Humbert Phillips*.

Mock trials are also done in law schools, and you will have an opportunity to participate in one here. The legal issues are complex, and good arguments are available on all sides. We revisit the notions of paternalism (first discussed in chap. 2) and intent (discussed in the *Crime and Punishment* section of this chapter) here. You may wish to contemplate the mysterious ideas of *wrongless harm* and *harmless wrong,* which come into play here.

Wrongless harm refers to harm or injury done for which no one is to blame. *Harmless wrong* refers to wrongdoing that really doesn't hurt anyone. Can you think of some examples of each?

Procedure

There are three steps: (1) reading, (2) discussion questions, and (3) the trial. The procedure for the trial will follow the discussion questions.

1. Read the case and do the discussion questions for homework. As a class, you will retell the story from memory. One person starts, then another will continue, until all the relevant facts are told. If someone forgets something, please interrupt and add the missing information.

2. For the discussion questions that follow the case, circle the answer you feel is best. If you don't like any of the answers, write your own answer at the last letter (e or f). In class you will discuss your answers and try to convince the others that your answer is best. We will use a *Scoring System* to encourage you to fight for your answer as the best.

   2 points if your original answer is the same as the answer that the majority decides upon after discussion

   1 point if you change your mind and agree with the majority

   0 if you are in the minority and do not change your mind

   0 for everyone if there is no majority

Vocabulary Gloss

dirty old man	=	morally corrupt, sexually perverse man
frostbite	=	freezing of some body part
not much of a	=	not a very good
ad	=	advertisement
eccentric	=	behaving in a not ordinary way
granted	=	given
nude	=	naked, without clothing
had the police in his pocket	=	controlled the police because of money and/or power
snooping	=	searching in improper or illegal manner
blackmail	=	getting money or forcing someone to do something, by threat of public exposure or threat of harm
trespassing	=	going onto private property without permission
battery	=	attack, violently harming someone

The Case of Humbert Phillips

Humbert Phillips is an angry, unhappy, and very rich old man. Some say he is a sick and *dirty old man*° as well. He lives on Cape Cod and is a neighbor to the Kennedys. His dream, as a young man, was to climb Mt. Everest. Not only did he fail in the attempt, but he lost three toes to *frostbite.*° This has left him permanently bitter. And he is *not much of a* ° dancer.

Climbing Mt. Everest is a very challenging and dangerous undertaking. The chances of death or some permanent damage from frostbite are near 50%. Humbert Phillips has reason to be proud of his attempt to climb Everest, but he feels humiliated by his failure.

He has several times put an *ad*° in climbing magazines. It reads as follows.

Eccentric° millionaire will pay $10,000 to anyone who climbs to the top of Mt. Everest during the next month and can prove it.

Although one month was not much time to prepare for the climb, numerous climbers were enthusiastic at the opportunity to make a large sum of money doing what they enjoyed most. And many incompetent climbers were tempted by the money to make the climb. The result was that every time the ad went in, several climbers died. And a total of about 100 toes and fingers were lost to frostbite in just two years.

This delighted Phillips, who admitted in newspaper interviews that he did it just to see others suffer. Because the injury rate from these attempts was so high, many politicians were advocating a law making it a crime to climb Mt. Everest without a license. This license would not be *granted*° within one month and would only be granted to very experienced climbers.

Two more reporters, James Roberts and Lana Langer, wanted to write another story about Phillips. Phillips refused to talk to them, so they had to use

Numerous climbers were enthusiastic at the opportunity to make a large sum of money doing what they enjoyed most.

some unconventional methods to get their story. There was a locked gate on the driveway to his large estate, so they drove their Jeep through some heavy brush, which Phillips had found too difficult to clear, instead of going up the driveway. The two reporters would do anything to get their story.

What they saw was Phillips sunbathing *nude*° on his private beach. But many people walked, legally, through the surf to get from the public beach on one side to the public beach on the other side. Nobody had objected to his nudity, perhaps because people were afraid that Phillips, who was rich and powerful, *had the police in his pocket.*°

Phillips discovered the reporters and asked them to come into his house. He then thanked them for clearing a path to the beach. And while he was getting some refreshments, James and Lana made a startling discovery. In a closet were hundreds of fingers and toes that Phillips had paid some people who lived near Mt. Everest a lot of money for.

Phillips again discovered the *snooping*° reporters and agreed to talk to them about his *collection,* but separately. What he didn't notice was that a dozen toes were missing. James had stuffed them into his pockets. He would have taken them all if Phillips hadn't appeared. Later, James threw them into the sea.

Phillips talked privately to Lana, who said, "I'm going to tell the police about your collection and your nude sunbathing."

Phillips said, "Wait. Don't do that. If you don't tell anyone, I will give you $10,000." Lana was silent for a minute, and Phillips raised the offer to $20,000, which she accepted.

"Of course you'll use your influence with that young Roberts boy, won't you?" he said.

Lana smiled, and Phillips sent her away. Then he spoke to James, who said, "Give up this practice of offering a reward for climbing Everest or I'll tell the police about your collection and about your nude sunbathing, which is against the law."

Phillips said, "I'll think about it, but in Nepal, where I'm going for a long vacation. The plane leaves in one hour, so I've got to hurry. So long."

He got into his Rolls Royce and was about to close the door. James said, "Let me help you," and he slammed the door on Phillips' fingers, breaking all of them.

Phillips went to the hospital instead of going on vacation. And ironically, the plane that Phillips was going to take crashed, killing all on board.

The next day, Humbert Phillips was arrested for *indecent exposure* (nude sunbathing). Lana and James say they didn't tell the police. They say that someone else must have complained, perhaps one of his wealthy neighbors.

Phillips, for his part, insisted that the two reporters be arrested for theft, *blackmail,*° *trespassing,*° and *battery.*°

Discussion Questions

1. Are Lana and James guilty of trespassing?
    a. Yes. They drove their Jeep onto Phillips's property without permission.
    b. No. They improved his property by creating a path to the beach, which Phillips wanted. They did him a favor.
    c. No. Lana and James did Phillips a favor. He should compensate them.
    d. Yes, but there should be no fine or punishment.
    e.

2. Is Lana guilty of blackmail?
   a. Yes. She got Phillips to pay her $20,000 to keep quiet.
   b. No. She didn't ask for money. He offered it. She didn't threaten to talk unless he paid. She is only exercising her right to free speech.
   c. Yes, because she clearly was blackmailing him. If she didn't intend to blackmail him, why did she accept the money?
   d. Yes, especially because she agreed to use her influence on James to make him keep quiet too.
   e.

3. Is James guilty of blackmail?
   a. Yes. He is forcing Phillips to do something by threat of public exposure.
   b. No. You cannot blackmail a person into doing good. James's threat is legal and morally good because it makes Phillips a better person.
   c. Yes, but there should be no punishment.
   d. No, unless he accepts some of Lana's $20,000 and keeps silent.
   e.

4. Should nude sunbathing in public be considered a crime?
   a. Yes. It offends general public morality. If your mother or some small children saw him, they would be shocked.
   b. No. Why should a naked body be considered immoral?
   c. No. Perhaps it offends some people's sense of morality, but they can't force their morality on others.
   d. No. If people don't like it, they don't have to look, or they can go somewhere else.
   e. No. It may be immoral, but no one is harmed by it.
   f.

5. Supposing that nude sunbathing in public is a crime (indecent exposure), is Phillips guilty of it?
   a. Yes. Phillips knew that people would walk through the surf and see him.
   b. No. You can do what you want on your own private property.
   c. No. People who are offended by nude sunbathing can go from one public beach to the other via the road, although it is longer than walking through the surf.
   d. No. People don't have to look if they are offended.
   e.

6. Should "toe collecting" be considered a crime?

    a. Yes. It encourages criminals to chop off the toes of living people.
    b. Yes. It encourages the mutilation of the corpses of people who were loved. How would you like it if the toes of your dead relative were chopped off?
    c. No. Encouraging is not forcing; it is not a crime.
    d. Yes. It encourages poor people to sell their own toes.
    e. No. If people are stupid enough to sell their own body parts, that's their business. Besides, it is legal in most states to sell your blood, and legal everywhere to sell your hair for wigs.
    f.

7. Is James guilty of theft?
    a. Yes. He stole Phillips's property—a dozen toes.
    b. No. The toes were never Phillips's property but the property of the climbers who lost them ("finders, keepers" does not apply).
    c. Yes. Phillips paid about $120,000 for those toes to people who worked to get them. If the climbers wanted to keep their toes when they were amputated, why didn't they say so?
    d. No. It is not a crime to take away property that is illegally acquired.
    e. No, because James didn't sell them but threw them away, for moral reasons.
    f.

8. Is James guilty of battery?
    a. Yes. He deliberately broke Phillips's fingers.
    b. No. He was preventing the escape of a criminal.
    c. Yes. It is the business of the police to deal with criminals, not the public. Phillips hadn't been arrested, so he had a right to travel wherever he liked.
    d. No. He saved Phillips's life. Phillips would have died in the plane crash if James had not broken his fingers. Phillips should thank him.
    e.

9. Should the law referred to in paragraph 5 of the story be passed?
    a. Yes. This law would prevent deaths and much toe loss, and it would not hamper serious climbers.
    b. No. This is grossly paternalistic. No one should be able to interfere with another person's liberty to climb any mountain he or she wants.
    c. No. Although the purpose of the law is good, there is too much room for abuse of the law; that is, who determines what "very experienced" means, and how do you prove that you are "very experienced"?
    d. No. Climbers are encouraged to do something heroic, which is great if successful, and they are compensated generously if they fail—they can sell their own toes and fingers to Phillips.
    e.

Trial Procedure

For homework, selected students will prepare the roles of James, Lana, and Humbert. We will hold a trial the next day but with some radical differences from normal trials. The teacher is the judge and will practice benign neglect. The rest of the class is the jury, who will decide the outcome. All the students (jurors) will erase all memory of the case and *ask questions* of the defendants. There will be no lawyers and no prosecutor. Defendants will accuse each other and will defend themselves. One way for the trial to begin is for the judge to ask, "Who has a complaint?" During this recounting of discontent, all the facts of the case should come to light. Of course, there will be disagreement over the "facts."

Defendants should deny wrongdoing, convincingly. Also, they should think of imaginative ways to explain that the crime is not attributable to them. In other words, they should think of valid excuses.

Finally, we will break into several groups (*juries*) and in five to ten minutes reach a verdict for all parties. If the class is small, just one jury may be formed. While the jurors deliberate (quickly), the teacher will point out to the players some of the mistakes they made in grammar and pronunciation and thank them for their efforts.

The order of charges the jury will take up will be as follows.

1. *Indecent Exposure* (nude sunbathing). Defendant—Phillips

2. *Trafficking in Body Parts.* Defendant—Phillips

3. *Trespassing.* Defendants—James, Lana

4. *Blackmail.* Defendants—James, Lana

5. *Battery.* Defendant—James

The judge will divide the time so that all charges will be taken up. In order for there to be a guilty verdict on any charge, the vote must be unanimous.

Writing Assignment

Write your opinion on one or more of the charges.

The International View

What issues in your country does this case bring up? (For example, is it ever legal, under any circumstances, for a person to sell part of his or her body?)

6

Linguistics

You Don't Understand Me

When men and women agree, it's only in
their conclusions; their reasons always differ.
                    —George Santayana

Objectives

to understand that miscommunication between the sexes comes in part
from the fact that men and women speak, in effect, different languages

to interpret ordinary speech (*reading between the lines*)

Introduction

You will find in college that linguistics intersects with many disciplines. Here, we will see how linguistics intersects with psychology. You will look beneath the surface meaning of the language, which is something you will have to do in studying literature and other subjects.

We often joke that men and women do not speak the same language. But some psychologists and linguists are taking this joke seriously. They say that there exist, in effect, *genderlects*—dialects spoken and understood among men or among women but not between men and women. Of course men and women in America speak the same language, English, but how each sex, or gender, communicates is more easily understood by others of the same gender.

Though not much research has been done regarding other languages, it is reasonable to suspect that the same phenomenon of misunderstanding between genders occurs everywhere. Think about whether the following scenarios could occur in your country. Think about incidents you have experienced or know about where there was misunderstanding due to this genderlect phenomenon and relate these to your class.

Vocabulary Gloss

bewildered   =   confused, puzzled
nibble   =   eat a very small bit
wolfing down   =   eating very rapidly
nope   =   no
adultery   =   sexual intercourse between a married person and someone
                    other than his or her spouse
eats   =   bothers (slang)

Procedure

Read each exercise and write your answer to the question that follows.   The
class, as a whole, will discuss their answers.
Compare the differences, if any, between men's interpretations and women's.

Exercise 1
Rhett and Carla O'Hara went to a movie, as they often did on Friday nights.

> *Carla:*   Do you want to get some popcorn?

> *Rhett:*   (truthfully) No.

Driving home after the very long Civil War movie, Carla did not say anything,
which was unusual. Rhett knew she was upset, but he couldn't figure out why.
"I'll never understand women," he said to himself.

Question. Why was Carla upset? Did she have good reason to be upset?

Answer

Exercise 2
Henry and Cordelia MacDuff were walking home. Cordelia noticed that Henry
was limping slightly, and she asked why. He said that he'd hurt his ankle playing
volleyball. She asked when it happened, and he said, "About two weeks ago."
Cordelia seemed to be irritated. Henry was *bewildered.* What had he done?

Question. Why was Cordelia irritated? Did she have good reason to be irritated?

Answer

Exercise 3

Miranda is frustrated and upset with her husband Prospero. She relates these recent conversations to her therapist, Dr. Joy.

> *Miranda:* What time is the performance?
>
> *Prospero:* You have to be ready by eight-thirty.
>
> *Miranda:* How many guests did you invite to our party tonight?
>
> *Prospero:* Don't worry. I got enough wine.

Question. Why is Miranda frustrated and upset? Is there anything wrong with Prospero's responses to her questions?

Answer

Exercise 4

Clea and her husband Anthony are about to go to sleep, and she tells him about what has been bothering her.

> *Clea:* I don't know how to get along with my mother. I felt so abandoned as a kid. She worked all the time and never had any time for me. And now she laughs about how busy she was back then and how neglected I must have felt. But I know she feels guilty, and that's why she drinks too much. But I don't know how to talk to her. It makes me feel so sad.
>
> *Anthony:* Go up there this weekend. Tell her about all those incidents in your childhood that made you feel bad. And suggest that she join Alcoholics Anonymous, to get some help with her drinking.

(Clea rolled away, onto her side, and said no more, but Anthony could tell that she was crying. He didn't understand why she didn't continue the conversation and work out a plan of what to do.)

Question. Why is Anthony bewildered, wondering why Clea is upset with him? He thinks that all he did was to try to help her solve her problem.

Answer

Exercise 5

It was Friday night and the second anniversary of Orson and Marilyn Goode. They decided just to go to the movies, which they both loved doing. Marilyn eats a lot but does not like to admit it.

> *Orson:* Want any popcorn?
>
> *Marilyn:* I'm not really hungry.
>
> *Orson:* I could eat a horse. But I guess I'll settle for a small popcorn. Want anything to drink?
>
> *Marilyn:* No. Why don't you get a medium, and I'll just *nibble**?

Orson bought a medium buttered popcorn for $3.50 and was angry about the cost (small—$2.25; large—$4.75). He was hungry, and when he got angry he got hungrier. They sat down, and he began, as Marilyn saw it, *wolfing down** the popcorn. The movie would not start for another five minutes, and it was half gone. She always waited for the movie to start before she ate any popcorn.

> *Marilyn:* Do you think we should save some for when the movie starts?
>
> *Orson:* *Nope.** Want some?

Marilyn shook her head and looked through her bag for a piece of gum. When they left, Marilyn was unusually silent and seemed to Orson to be in a bad mood. He was very disappointed because he wanted this to be a happy occasion.

Question. Why was Marilyn in a bad mood? Should she have been?

Answer

Exercise 6

Rhett and Carla have been *seeing* a marriage counselor, Dr. Joy. She has told Rhett to be more open about what bothers him, to confront issues rather than to swallow them so that his anger doesn't build internally and then explode over some small issue. It's Friday night, and Rhett proposes that they see a movie, *The Scarlet Pimpernel.*

Carla: What's it about?

Rhett: Adultery° or prostitution, I think. I'm not sure. I read the book a long time ago, in high school.

Carla: I think I read it too.

Rhett: Yeah, it was pretty neat. Maybe it was about the French Revolution.

Carla: Do you know what's playing at the Regent?

Rhett: I didn't check.

Carla: Did you know that the Coolidge Corner Cinema is having a French movie festival?

Rhett: Yeah, I think they have it every year. It's kind of an annual thing. The movie starts at 7:00. We can make it if we leave now.

When they get to the movie, *The Scarlet Pimpernel*, Rhett remembers what Dr. Joy said, and he follows her advice.

Rhett: Carla, can I share something with you? One thing that *eats*° me is that we always get a medium popcorn, and I don't feel satisfied with half. Or maybe I'm just possessive. I mean, you hold the popcorn on your knee and I have to reach over, and I want to hold it. If I don't, I feel insecure. So, just so you know, I mean, I'm going to buy a small popcorn, for me. You want one?

Carla: No.

Rhett: Sure? Why the sad face? Did I say something wrong?

Carla: Frankly, my dear, you just don't understand!

Question. Why is Carla sad? Did Rhett say something wrong?

Answer

The International View

What differences do you find, if any, between men's and women's conversation in your native language?

Arranging the Marriage of Indira and Raphael
(An Indirect Speech Exercise)

Objectives

mastery of sequence of tenses used in indirect speech (this is essential for successful discussion and negotiation)

cross-cultural ideas of a good marriage partner and how marriage might be arranged

Introduction

Students should prepare by thinking about the following questions, which will be discussed in class before doing the activity.

1. Is there a dowry in your country? If so, who pays it, the woman's or man's family?

2. Do marriage customs vary from city to countryside?

3. What are the roles of the man's and the woman's family in a marriage?

4. What are some marriage customs in your country? In the United States, the bride wears "something old, something new, something borrowed, something blue." She throws a bouquet of flowers to the women and a garter to the men; those who catch these should have luck getting married soon. Rice is thrown. Sometimes friends will try to steal the bride's or groom's clothes before they depart for their honeymoon.

5. Are marriages sometimes arranged in your country?

Vocabulary Gloss

dowry = money or goods traditionally given as a condition of marriage, usually from the bride's family to the groom's

caste = rigid class division in society

Arranging the Marriage of Indira and Raphael

Imagine the following situation, which takes place in a fictional country that we will call Nadur.

Raphael is a thirty-five-year-old man who has not married.
Indira is a beautiful seventeen-year-old girl who is finishing high school.

Raphael

Raphael is a thirty-five-year-old man who has never married. He has given in to his parents' insistence and has agreed that it is time to find a wife. His parents are very rich, and they demand a substantial *dowry.** He works in the bank owned by his father. His family belongs to the country's highest *caste.**

Indira

Indira is a beautiful seventeen-year-old girl who is finishing high school. She has gone to private girls' schools all her life. She comes from the caste just below Raphael's. She loves her parents but has talked about running away to become an actress.

Procedure

You will be divided into two or four groups representing either Raphael's family or Indira's family. Each family will have one interlocutor, who will practice indirect speech. Indirect speech is the reporting of what someone has said. For example,

> *John:* "She is nice."   (direct speech)
>
> John said that she was nice.   (indirect speech)

"That" in indirect speech is often omitted. Notice too that the tense of the verb *to be* backshifts, that is, it changes to a tense further in the past.
  Other changes that are essential for this exercise are

> *can*—changes to *could*
>
> *will*—changes to *would*
>
> *must*—changes to *had to*

Useful structures

> They said (that)
>
> She asked if
>
> They asked whether
>
> They told me that

Note

We often ignore the changes made in indirect speech when the time between the speaking and the reporting is very short. For instance,

> *John:* "It is 12:00." (direct speech)
>
> a. John *said* that it *was* 12:00. (indirect speech)
>
> b. John said that it *is* 12:00. (indirect speech)

a is formally correct. The verb *is* was changed to the simple past tense to agree with "said", which is in the simple past tense. However, if the reporting is done almost immediately, *b* is acceptable. In fact, most native speakers of English would say *b*. In this exercise, you will try to speak formally, making as many changes as are practical.

It is a custom in Nadur that the families of the man and woman to be wed do not speak directly to each other. So the arranging of this marriage has to be done indirectly.

1. The family of Raphael will meet and invent the details and history of their son (or cousin, etc.). You should include the following.
   a. his educational background
   b. detailed physical description (including flaws—it is said that he is not terribly handsome)
   c. explanation of why he is unmarried at 35
   d. what you want for a dowry
   e. his hobbies, interests, political leanings, habits (good and bad), likes, dislikes

2. The family of Indira will simultaneously meet and invent the details and history of their daughter (or cousin, etc.). You should include the following.
   a. information on her parents and family
   b. detailed physical description
   c. hobbies, interests, political leanings, habits (good and bad), likes, dislikes
   d. her goals in life
   e. what you wish to give as a dowry

3. The teacher will then give each group different rumors about Raphael and Indira. You must investigate these rumors.

4. The interlocutors will just listen in on the first stage of discussion. Then they will relay questions and answers back and forth between the families, who

must be at some distance apart. Two interlocutors are necessary so that both families will be constantly busy either answering or asking. Sometimes both interlocutors will be with the same family, but the teacher will speed one along to the other family. The interlocutors must use indirect speech, which the teacher will monitor.

Presentation

The teacher may ask one or more of you to prepare a presentation on wedding customs in your country. Your classmates will have many questions for you, and they may compare or contrast wedding customs in their countries.

The International View

(See the five questions in the introduction to this section.)

Conditionally Speaking

Objectives

to understand the larger semantic issues of conditionals

to see that linguistics can be fun as well as challenging

to understand speech acts

to introduce the relation of logic and conditionals

Introduction

As students, you learn rules regarding the use of conditionals, but you normally are not exposed to the debate that goes on in linguistics over basic issues, such as what a conditional is. In this author's view, the jury is still out. Conditionals normally express a relation between two clauses, but just what that relation consists of is not clear. And in fact, a conditional may be expressed with only one clause. You will see also that conditionals may be expressed without an "if." Dealing with conditionals in this nontraditional way should be interesting and fun. By looking at conditionals in a different way, we may achieve the goal of using them competently and may also have some fun in the process.

Vocabulary Gloss

| donkey | = | animal similar to a horse, with large ears |
| stubborn | = | not responsive to suggestions |

Procedure

Answer as many of the following questions as you can. Some questions demand that you write a sentence or two. In small groups, you will compare your answers and explain your ideas to the other students. One is a matter of life or death!

1. Do these sentences mean the same thing? If not, explain the difference.
   a. If *donkeys*° are slow in Spain, Raúl beats them.
   b. If Spanish donkeys are slow, Raúl beats them.

2. Do these sentences mean essentially the same thing? If not, explain the difference.

   If donkeys have green eyes, they are *stubborn.*°

   Donkeys that have green eyes are stubborn.

   Donkeys with green eyes are stubborn.

   Green-eyed donkeys are stubborn.

3. The following statement is true: Donkeys are stubborn if they have green eyes, and they are stupid if they have brown eyes.
   (True or False) Donkeys cannot be stubborn *and* stupid.

4. Is there a difference between
   a. If you open your refrigerator, it won't explode.
   and
   b. If you open your refrigerator, *then* it won't explode.

5. The butler doesn't have mud on his shoes. If the butler is the murderer, he left by the window. If he left by the window, he has mud on his shoes. Is the butler the murderer?

6. *Speech Acts and Conditionals*

Speech acts include offers, promises, denials, rewards or inducements, threats or warnings, appeals or requests. In the following two examples, you will decide what kind of speech acts are being used, and you will decide what the relationship is between the listener and the speaker. This is tricky: there may be more than one answer!

(*Note:* a C is an average grade, not good and not bad.)

a. "Marry my daughter and I'll give you a C."

The speaker is a _____(profession).

The listener is a (good/bad) _____.

The speech act is _____.

b. "Marry my daughter or I'll give you a C."

The speaker is a _____(profession).

The listener is a (good/bad) _____.

The speech act is _____.

The International View

How are conditionals in your native language different from conditionals in English?

Presentation

If you are interested in linguistics, you may ask the teacher if you can do a presentation of conditionals in your language, perhaps explaining how they differ from English conditionals.

7

Business Negotiation

Freeloaders

Objectives

to understand more fully the concept of compensation

to see how different cultures show differences of strictness in regulating social conformity

Introduction

In this section, we will discuss the idea of compensation in a context that might surprise you—lawn care. This issue also is at the heart of the business case that appears in the next section, *The Great Bun Caper.* Compensation crosses into the realm of philosophy as well. Because compensation should be just, it is a matter of distributive justice. The concept enters into many business practices, for instance when laying off people.

Vocabulary Gloss

bountiful	=	producing a lot of (usually about fruit or crops)
prized	=	highly esteemed
gourmets	=	people who know and love good food
dummy	=	stupid person
lawn	=	grassy area (usually mowed)
mowed	=	cut (said of grass or lawn)
laissez-faire	=	doctrine of letting things alone, not interfering or regulating (borrowed from French)

Procedure

You will write and hand in a one-paragraph answer to each of the questions that follow. In class, in small groups, you will exchange views on each of the questions. When you are finished, the teacher will elicit from the class as a whole what the general opinion seems to be.

1. Mr. Chu has an apple tree. It is a *bountiful** tree. But many of the apples fall over the fence into Mr. King's yard. Can Mr. Chu climb the fence and pick up the apples? Can Mr. King make a pie from the apples even if Mr. Chu shouts, "Give them back!"?

2. As it turns out, these are the best apples in the state. They are *prized** by *gourmets** everywhere, who will pay a lot for *Chu Apples*. Mr. King, no *dummy,** realizes their value, so he sells the ones that fall into his yard and makes a nice profit. Mr. Chu demands compensation. Should he get it? If so, how much should he get?

Mr. King, no dummy, sells the apples that fall into his yard.

3. The citizens of Eastwick have almost unanimously agreed that everybody must keep his or her *lawn** *mowed** to a uniform length of three inches. The one exception is Jack. He is an individualist. He dislikes government inter-ference in his affairs. He hates taxes and is always late in paying them. Jack lets his lawn grow untended and wild. The grass is nearly two feet tall. Even Jack thinks it is kind of ugly, but his philosophy is *laissez-faire** in everything. And he just doesn't like anybody telling him what to do.

Walking down the street, however, Jack is impressed at how uniformly beautiful the lawns are. Their beauty makes him smile and feel good. The property value for the whole neighborhood has certainly increased since the neighbors agreed to keep their lawns in perfect shape.

Now the neighbors are suing Jack for compensation. Although Jack has broken no law, the neighbors say he has unfairly profited from their agreement. They say that he is a freeloader.

Should Jack have to pay them compensation?

The International View

In your country, are there enforceable standards for property neatness? In other words, are people legally required to keep their property neat?

The Great Bun Caper

Objectives

to analyze a business problem and to make recommendations for further course of action

to learn to write a business memo

to deal with the problem of fair compensation in a profit-oriented environment

to make difficult but commonsense personnel decisions

to practice negotiating skills

to practice presentation skills

to analyze "the books"

Introduction

This is the first of two business cases dealing with problems within the framework of hamburger franchises. A *franchisee* is a person who pays a yearly sum to the parent company, or *franchisor*, for the right to sell a product. A contract spells out the fine points of the agreement, such as responsibility for paying advertising costs (which is one of the subjects of dispute in these cases).

Vocabulary Gloss

team player	=	cooperative, not egotistical, person
maverick	=	very individualistic person
sponsored	=	gave money for an activity, in return for publicity
out of my own pocket	=	I paid for it myself
altruistic	=	totally concerned with others, not egotistical
civic	=	relating to responsibility as a citizen
go 50/50	=	divide the cost evenly
backfired	=	had the reverse of the desired effect
dropping in on	=	visiting, perhaps spontaneously
hordes	=	large crowds
windfall	=	sudden and unexpected gain
shell out	=	reluctantly pay for
to his chagrin	=	(his) feeling embarrassed or humiliated
zealousness	=	passionate pursuit
mediate	=	to reconcile parties in dispute

Procedure

Two students will be assigned to *present* the case. One will present the facts of the case; the other will present the negotiation game. All students will read each case, but the presenters have the task of knowing all the vocabulary and understanding all facets of the case so that they can answer students' questions on it. The teacher will meet before class with the presenters to answer any questions they might have.

After the game is finished, students will fill out a *Peer Feedback Sheet* for each presenter. (A reproducible copy of this sheet appears at the end of *The Cow Dung Gaffe* section in this chapter.) These sheets will be collected (unsigned) and given to the presenters. The presenters' homework is to reflect on and analyze the data, then write a short paragraph on the topic "What I Can Do to Improve Next Time," summing up the feedback.

Special notes on the objectives and procedure of the game will follow the reading.

The Great Bun Caper

Adams and Banks run Hamburger Heaven franchises in the town of Eastwick. The franchises are a mile apart. The two men do not get along well, as they have very different managerial styles and personalities. Recently, Adams was so upset at Banks that he called the District Representative (DR) to complain.

The guy (Banks) is not a *team player.* Everyone knows that. I admit he makes a lot of money, a lot more than I do, and that is maybe what HH (Hamburger Heaven) is looking for, but he is a *maverick,* and in the long run I don't think that helps anybody. For example, last year I *sponsored* a Little League baseball team—*out of my own pocket.* It cost me $500, but it is advertising too. I mean, the team I sponsored won the city championship, and they had their pictures in the paper with Hamburger Heaven uniforms, and everybody ate at my shop after the game. So my sponsorship was not entirely *altruistic.* I got something out of it, but I also did it out of some kind of *civic* spirit. I asked Banks if he wanted to go *50/50* on the sponsorship, and he rejected the idea. I went ahead with it anyway. He realized just as much profit from the advertising and the good image as I did, but he did not contribute one cent.

Adams is a resourceful and entrepreneurial guy, with a talent for promotion. Some of his ideas have *backfired;* some have been described as crazy by the previous DR. The most disastrous was filling the franchise with balloons with a picture of a burger on them. Kids kept popping the balloons, irritating some of the clients and startling others. Nonetheless, Hamburger Heaven (HH) has been by and large supportive of local initiative in promotion, especially since the funding comes from the franchisee.

Popular singer James Tyler was a high school friend of Adams. On August 1, Tyler gave a concert on Cape Cod, after which he took a short vacation, *dropping in on* his old friend Adams.

Adams convinced Tyler to give a free promotional concert on the Boy Scout field. Adams paid $500 for a one-time ad on the local radio station telling about the concert.

The concert was well attended, and business for that day was 20% higher than normal, due mainly to the *hordes* of hungry people leaving the field by one of the paths that led through Adams's parking lot.

Since Banks's franchise was equidistant from the concert site, he received a similar *windfall,* nearly 20% higher sales volume than predicted—for which he contributed nothing. When questioned by DR, Banks replied:

Adams never asked me for a dime, but if he had, I wouldn't have given him one. I *shell out* 1% of my gross revenues to HH for advertising—that is considerably more than what Adams pays because I make a hell of a lot more than he does. Hey, if the wind blows the apples from his tree into my yard, am I forbidden to eat them? The fact is, I don't like James Tyler. His music is lousy, and his politics are worse. He is anti–atomic energy, and that is anti-American as far as I'm concerned. I don't think we want HH associated with that kind of guy.

DR thought about Banks's point of view as he sat down to french fries and a burger with extra cheese. And he had much more to contemplate, for Adams was giving him an additional headache. Anticipating a 30% increase in sales for the concert day, Adams had ordered 30% more burgers, but when the delivery truck arrived, he realized *to his* great *chagrin** that he had forgotten to order the corresponding increase in buns. Knowing that Banks compulsively overstocked, Adams unloaded from the delivery truck 30% more buns than he had ordered, buns which were to have been delivered to Banks.

Adams rationalized that (1) Banks would not be too upset, since he always had a large stock on hand and had probably again ordered more than he needed; (2) his need justified taking matters into his own hands; (3) the net benefit to HH would be greater; (4) if he asked Banks, his unfriendly competitor would certainly refuse; and (5) he would fairly compensate Banks for any loss incurred due to these actions.

After listening to Adams's story, DR called Banks and asked if he had any rebuttal to what seemed a well-reasoned action. Banks replied:

> Yeah, I have a couple of things to say to that. First, my oversupply was not sufficient to my demand—Adams was plain wrong about that. Second, it was not just the monetary loss from running out of buns, it was the embarrassment. How would you like to tell a customer that he cannot have a burger because there aren't any buns? And about cooperating? Hey, if you walk through Harvard Square and hear some street musicians you have no obligation to pay them, even if you like the music.

Out of buns, Banks was furious. He called Adams and complained. Adams was apologetic. When his store closed, he went to Banks's franchise and examined the books. Banks admitted that most of the customers who were refused burgers switched their orders to fries, chicken, or other items. A very small number actually walked out. Calculating this, Adams offered what he thought to be fair compensation to Banks.

But DR's further problem was that Banks insisted that HH punish Adams for his theft. On the one hand, it seemed that Adams's actions deserved to be discouraged, for as Banks pointed out, if this became standard practice, chaos would result.

But DR was reluctant to discourage the kind of local creative promotion that Adams had come up with. The Tyler concert would have cost HH more than $20,000.

But despite his *zealousness*,* Adams had only averaged about $60,000 per year from his franchise, while Banks had averaged $100,000, with a stronger upward curve in earnings. DR did not want to alienate his best franchisee. And while he was chewing on this problem along with some fries, Sonny Berger, the regional manager, called and asked DR to send him a memo explaining how he (DR) was going to deal with "the great bun caper."

Relevant Data from Banks's Books

	Total Sales	Sales of Items Requiring Buns	Sales of Items without Buns	Drinks
199– Ave./day	$2,000	$1,200	$400	$400
9/12/9–	$2,800	$1,500	$700	$600

[9/12/9– was the date of the concert]

["Sales of items without buns" means food items such as apple pies, french fries, frozen yogurt, eggs, etc.]

Adams unloaded from the delivery truck 30% more buns than he had ordered.

Negotiation Game

Objectives

Banks—to obtain the greatest amount of compensation and to convince DR to punish Adams for his theft

Adams—to pay the least amount of compensation

DR—to *mediate*° the dispute in a way that makes everybody happy and that will appear to Sonny Berger to be wise and good for business

Procedure

The class will be divided into groups of three, with each student in every group being assigned one of three roles—Adams, Banks, or DR.
Based on the case and your analysis of the "Relevant Data from Banks's Books," each player will argue his or her case. You will have a predetermined amount of time (around 20 min.) in which a decision *must* be made by DR.

Memos

Each player is required to write a one-page (250 words) memo to Sonny Berger. Assume that Berger has been fairly well informed about the facts of the case, so these need not be repeated. The memo will concern the results of the negotiation. One way to organize the memo is to use the following setup: one short paragraph with background *and* the decision; one paragraph summarizing Adams's arguments; one paragraph summarizing Banks's arguments; one paragraph on how DR decided to mediate; one paragraph appraising DR's decision. (If you are Adams or Banks, bear in mind that DR will probably see your memo and that you must continue working with him in the future.)

Note: Memos, as opposed to reports, are short and to the point, with no rhetorical flourishes. They do not begin with "Dear" and do not have a closing. Follow this form.

> Date:
> *To:*   Sonny Berger, Regional Mgr., Hamburger Heaven
> *From:*   (*Adams,* or *Banks*, or *DR* —then add your own name)
> *Re***:**   The Great Bun Caper

The International View

Does your country respect "mavericks"? Do they have a place in your business culture? Or is there only room for "team players"?

The Cow Dung Gaffe

Objectives

> to deal with a difficult personnel dilemma
>
> to negotiate from strength
>
> to practice role playing
>
> to practice business memo writing
>
> to practice presentation skills

Vocabulary Gloss

irrepressible	=	impossible to restrain or control
gimmick	=	clever trick or stratagem
enclave	=	small, distinct community
leaflet	=	single sheet of paper with writing on it
gaffe	=	embarrassing mistake
dung	=	excrement
flop	=	failure
hottest	=	most popular or successful
bottom line	=	(accounting) final balance after computing revenues and expenses
gross	=	total income before deductions
roll out the carpet	=	treat someone's arrival with dignity
kick your butt	=	(slang) defeat you badly
dying to	=	(an infinitive) desiring strongly
no-win	=	having the appearance of doing badly no matter what happens
bluffing	=	pretending to be in strong position
upcoming	=	approaching (in time)

Procedure

Read the case carefully before class. One or two students will be assigned to *present* the case.

Then you will be assigned a role as Banks or DR and will negotiate for a predetermined time. Your goal is a settlement that is acceptable to both parties and that makes you look good.

After negotiating, you will have to write a one-page memo.

DR will write to Sonny Berger, Regional Manager, defending his actions. He will inform Berger of the outcome and discuss how it evolved. His actions should be justified as rational and as benefitting HH. In other words, he must show that he did the right thing.

Banks will write to Frank Chase, the outgoing president of the American Brotherhood of Independent Franchisees (ABIF). He must justify the outcome as fitting for a future president. In other words, he must make himself look good.

In both cases, you should assume that Berger and Chase are familiar with the background of the incident, so this only needs to be mentioned briefly.

The Cow Dung Gaffe

No sooner had DR sent his memo to Sonny Berger than the *irrepressible*° Adams undertook another promotional adventure that would profit him but not Banks. Adams realized that a large portion of the neighborhood just north of his franchise was Hispanic. From his own pocket he paid for some advertising on the local Spanish-language radio station. He had 50 copies of his menu printed up in Spanish and had them distributed by hand in the Hispanic neighborhood. Afterward, his sales increased 5% per month, an increase that seemed to Adams attributable only to his advertising. This conclusion was reinforced by his own observations that more Hispanic people were frequenting the restaurant and that there was an increase in applications for employment by Hispanic youths.

The story of Adams's success immediately spread to the other franchises, and among those first to learn of it was Banks. He immediately set about copying Adams's *gimmick.*° He realized that the neighborhood to the south of his franchise was densely populated by Vietnamese and Laotian refugees, and it had been for many years a Chinese-American *enclave.*° Though he could find no radio station broadcasting in the necessary languages, Banks paid for the same kind of *leaflet*° advertising that Adams had done. However, Banks's costs were three times as much, as he had to have menus prepared in three languages. To his chagrin, he found that the translator—a person who was fluent in Vietnamese and Laotian—made a *gaffe*° in Vietnamese that equated burgers to cow *dung.*°

The advertising proved to be a *flop.*° Sales in fact decreased slightly. Bitter, Banks deducted his personal advertising costs ($900) from the one percent of revenues due the franchisor at the end of the month.

When the franchisor telephoned Banks to ask for payment, Banks refused to pay the $900, adding that he had never liked the idea of paying the franchisor such a large sum of money for advertising, the fruit of which could never be adequately documented—in Banks's opinion.

When DR threatened him with the loss of his franchise, Banks responded:

> Go ahead, fire me. I have the *hottest*° franchise in Massachusetts. The *bottom line*° is—you'll lose as much as $100,000 *gross*° revenues if you replace me. Justify that to Sonny Berger! You know how he loves the bottom line like his mother. Fire me and I'll go to another hamburger chain. With my record, they'll *roll out the carpet*° for me. I'll open a franchise across the street from you and *kick your butt,*° and you know I can do it. I drove the Pizza House into bankruptcy—remember?

Sonny Berger wasted no time in calling DR, wondering what was going on in Massachusetts and why all of his headaches seemed to come from Eastwick. Adams and the other franchisees were waiting to see the outcome of the confrontation, as they were not happy paying 1% advertising to HH either. And Adams was *dying to*° do the same thing Banks had done—subtract his out-of-pocket advertising costs from the 1%.

It seemed a *no-win** situation to DR. But after some investigation, he found that Banks might just be *bluffing.** He had just bought a $200,000 house and had taken out a 20 year mortgage. Under these circumstances, would he really walk out? And would another hamburger chain really hire a guy who was fired for failing to fulfill his contractual obligations to the franchise?

DR tried to think of options. Was there a way to compromise? A deal he could make so that Banks might save face? This was important since Banks was a candidate for the *upcoming** election of the president of the American Brotherhood of Independent Franchisees (ABIF). The outgoing president, in effect, chose his successor, and Banks had felt he had a good chance at winning. But neither giving in nor getting fired would help his cause.

The International View

Banks needed to save face. Is losing face a very serious thing in your country?

Peer Feedback Sheet

(1 is best; 5 is worst. Circle your response)

1. Clarity of content (was the presentation clear?)
   1   2   3   4   5

2. Eye contact
   1   2   3   4   5

3. Pronunciation
   1   2   3   4   5

4. Pace
   S   S/E   E   E/F   F
   Slow   Excellent   Fast

(S/E is somewhere between Slow and Excellent. E/F is somewhere between Excellent and Fast.)

[This page is reproducible]

Laying Off at the Auto Plant (A Personnel Dilemma)

Objectives

> to examine our criteria for making difficult personnel decisions

> to attempt to solve a very practical business problem as an individual and as a committee member

Introduction

If you attend business school, you will have to explain your business decisions and defend them. In reality, these decisions are tough because they involve employees' well-being. As a member of a committee, you have a voice in the decision-making process and you have the responsibility for the decision. This may be frustrating, but it is a fact of life in a corporation.

Vocabulary Gloss

laid off	=	unemployed (not because of poor performance)
CEO	=	chief executive officer (head of the company)
(to get) walking papers	=	(slang) to lose your job
fainting spells	=	periods of falling unconscious

Personnel Dilemma

You are the supervisor of a division of an automobile factory (auto plant). The company is doing badly, and 25% of the work force must be *laid off.* Thus, one of the employees in your division must go, and the decision is entirely in your hands. To whom will you hand *walking papers?*

Procedure

You will read the case and make your decision for homework. Then in class you will meet in small groups. Present your decision and give your reasons. You are now the automobile company layoff recommendation committee. Your boss has demanded that you make a group decision today. The majority rules. When done, each group will defend its decision, briefly, to the class as a whole.

	Tom	Dick	Harriet	Rose
Seniority	25 yrs.	5 yrs.	20 yrs.	10 yrs.
Performance	good	excellent	fair/good	good
Wage	25/hr.	15/hr.	20/hr.	17/hr.
Age	50	24	39	30
Health	high blood pressure	exc., but calls in sick 3–4 times per month	unexplained *fainting spells*°	suffers from depression
Marital Status	divorced	single	divorced	married
Dependents	1 girl in last year of college	0	3 kids, ages 8, 15, 18	1 boy age 5
Miscellaneous	has filed several complaints about workplace safety	well-liked, captain of work baseball & basketball teams	ex-husband disappeared 5 yrs. ago and pays no child support	niece of the company president

The International View

Do workers get laid off in your country or is there a lifetime commitment from the company to the employees?

Writing Assignment

The higher you rise in a career in business, the more you will be making *policy* decisions.

Situation: You have been asked by the CEO of the auto company to create a policy paper on layoffs. Managers throughout the country will use this policy to determine whom to lay off. You must create criteria for laying off. What, for example, is the most crucial factor in the decision: seniority, performance, age? In your speaking exercise you had data for some factors, but you can think of others.

Part 1

Write a policy paper of one to two pages. Remember that you are giving directions to managers here. There should be no description of how difficult a task this is, no sympathy for the managers who find themselves in a difficult situation. You are trying to prevent managers from making bad decisions, based on foolish criteria, the outcome of which will alienate your workers.

Part 2

One student will be chosen as CEO. He or she will not have to write the policy paper. Instead, this student (the CEO) will collect the papers from all the students in the class. (If it is a large class, two CEOs will be chosen.) The CEO will read all the papers, then evaluate them. The CEO will write comments on the papers, praising them for insights and pointing out where the policy might be strengthened. In class, the CEO will single out one or two policy papers that were particularly insightful and explain why they were.

Notes to the Teacher

This text provides enough material for at least two semesters' work. Unless your class has a very specific academic preparation need, I would recommend that you choose those sections that appeal most to you rather than exhausting any one particular section.

The text has an academic orientation in terms of subject matter, but advanced classes with no specific academic orientation will also find the text very useful. Many of the topics are of general *cultural* interest. In fact, only the business negotiation section would have a limited audience. "Divorce," "Marital Issues," and "Paternalism," just to name a few topics, are issues of broad cultural interest.

The text gives students practice with phrases useful in carrying out speech functions. These phrases are labeled *Conversation Cues* and are discussed in the introduction to the student, then at greater length upon their first appearance, in the introductory exercise, *Roommate Search*. One way to proceed with these cues is to ask students to put a check mark next to a cue each time they use it. After the unit is finished, you may ask different students which ones they used most, or how often they used certain cues. Here is a list of those sections that contain *Conversation Cues* and the content of each set of cues.

Roommate Search (chap. 1):	*Stating Opinions, Suggestion*
The Desert Dilemma (chap. 2):	*Adding Information, Pointing out Irrelevancy*
Synergy (Lost At Sea) (chap. 3):	*Changing Your Mind, Asking for Repetition, Interruption*
The Race (chap. 4):	*Strong Disagreement*

If you are looking for a specific kind of activity, here is a partial list to help you locate what you are looking for.

Presentations	*Gender Attitudes (chap. 3); Rationality (Sunk Costs) (chap. 3); Synergy (Lost at Sea) (chap. 3); Mrs. Kerr and Ms. Pink (chap. 4); Crime and Punishment (chap. 5); Arranging the Marriage of Indira and Raphael (chap. 6); Conditionally Speaking (chap. 6); The Great Bun Caper (chap. 7); The Cow Dung Gaffe (chap. 7)*

Jigsaw	*The Desert Dilemma (chap. 2)*
Speeches	*Health Care—Providing Services to Visible and Invisible Victims (chap. 2)*
Writing	*Coercion/Paternalism (chap. 2); Paternalism in Action: American Laws (chap. 2); JFK Memorial Hospital versus Heston (chap. 2); Health Care—Rationing (chap. 2); Health Care—Providing Services to Visible and Invisible Victims (chap. 2); The Candy Bar Dilemma (chap. 4); The Race (chap. 4); The Case of Humbert Phillips (chap. 5); Freeloaders (chap. 7); The Great Bun Caper (chap. 7); The Cow Dung Gaffe (chap. 7)*
Interviews	*Rationality (Sunk Costs) (chap. 3); Survey (chap. 3)*
Cross-Cultural	*Marriage Cross-Culturally (chap. 3); You Don't Understand Me (chap. 6)*

For all of the exercises, the students should prepare before class. This allows more class time for discussion. If conserving time is not essential, many of the exercises can be started in class. You would need to look over the exercises beforehand to decide which you might prefer to do that way.

Some of the exercises that work well for less advanced classes can be done without prior preparation, especially with a dictation of the first paragraph or two. These include: *The Candy Bar Dilemma (Part 1)* (chap. 4); *The Race (Part 1)* (chap. 4); *Mrs. Kerr and Ms. Pink (Part 1)* (chap. 4); *Joe, His Bread, the Lifeboat (Part 1)* (chap. 4); *Sam and the Posse* (chap. 4).

It is my intention in this text to avoid rigidity and dogmatism in approach. You may see fit to modify the procedures with any exercise. For instance, if you want oral reports or group presentations, you could use the "Fugu" article that appears in the *Coercion/Paternalism* section of chapter 2 for these purposes. And all the exercises lend themselves to writing exercises, which you can easily add.

The sections entitled "The International View" that appear at the ends of the topics give students the opportunity to take the topics in any direction they want and to consider them from their own perspectives. These sections are meant to enhance cross-cultural communication and to give students an unstructured mode for discussion. This section can also be adapted, in almost all cases, to *presentations*.

Suggested Time is given for each section in the notes to the teacher. But different classes will need different amounts of time to finish any given unit.

Vocabulary is introduced by means of a gloss. There is an exercise in guessing meaning from context that appears in the *Coercion/Paternalism* section of chapter 2, but in a speaking text of this length, glossing is the only practical way to deal with vocabulary.

1. Introductory Exercise

Roommate Search: Categories and Ranking

Time: 30–40 min.

If your class has trouble coming up with ideas, you can use the list below, which I have compiled from many experiments with the exercise. And if your class is creating its own list, bear these categories in mind as ways to generalize the potential questions they might ask the potential roommate.

Category	*Personal Ranking*	*Group Ranking*
smoking	____	____
drugs	____	____
occupation	____	____
housework/neatness	____	____
food/cooking	____	____
interests/hobbies	____	____
politics	____	____
pets	____	____
style of life	____	____
religion	____	____

I usually include the category *gay/lesbian* among the questions for determining a suitable roommate. Clearly, not all teachers or classes will be comfortable dealing with it. I use it because I have found that the discussion is excellent. Some students find the idea unthinkable. Students are surprised to hear their peers say it wouldn't make any difference to them at all to have a gay roommate. This will be an eye-opener for many students, and exposing students to this viewpoint is something that I think is worthwhile.

You should ask students how many of the cues they used and which ones they used most often.

2. Ethics

Coercion/Paternalism

Time: 50 min.

Question 1. Teacher may act out—going to the window (assuming that there is one and it is not on the first floor) and telling students that he or she is going to jump. Tell them that the theory of gravity is a hoax, nonsense, and you will prove it to them.

Encourage students, in preparation for this section, to think of other things that the state might ban. Add these to questions 3–5, and then ask their groups their opinions.

Paternalism in Action: American Laws

Time: 40–60 min.
Question 5. In Massachusetts there are still "Blue Laws," left over from colonial times, that regulate conduct in ways we now find intolerable (e.g., no spitting on the sidewalk; no kissing in public).

JFK Memorial Hospital versus Heston

Time: 20–30 min.
The court ruled that the state has an interest in preserving life and could order the transfusion. It ruled that conduct in pursuit of religious beliefs could be regulated (what if they wanted to practice human sacrifice?).

Second, the hospital became an involuntary custodian of the patient. It had a duty to treat, which was stronger than the patient's right to die. It was unfair to ask a doctor to, in effect, kill the patient by operating without a transfusion.

In the past the court had ruled to order a transfusion for children of Jehovah's Witnesses when the parents didn't want it.

But in Illinois, the supreme court decided that a Jehovah's Witness did not have to have a transfusion. That person, the New Jersey court noted, did not have children who would become wards of the state. In any case, the New Jersey court decided that the state had an interest in preserving life and could order the transfusion.

(But consider this impossible scenario: the patient gets five pints of blood, and when he or she awakes, the doctor says, "We just gave you a transfusion, but there is a little plug that you can pull to let all the blood out. Good-bye." What would the patient do?)

You may wish to have students write an essay on this, expanding on the brief answer they wrote. The essay should be done after the discussion. You should instruct students to address the strongest contending views (which they have heard in the discussion) and argue forcefully against these contending views.

The Desert Dilemma

Time: 1½ hrs. for the entire activity. With some classes, when the discussion is lively, you can spend two hours or more.
Procedure: The teacher should read the following scenarios.
(Information that differs between scenarios is italicized.)

Group I
You are on an expedition to the Sahara desert. *It is a very hot place.* The expedition members are as follows: Professor Jones, the 50-year-old leader; William S. Benway, 40, *a physician who studied at Boston University;* two assistants; and a driver who is 34 years old and *has blue eyes.*

A few days ago, *on Monday,* you met a group of bedouin and agreed to take a woman who is *six months* pregnant and her two children, aged 12 and 13, to the nearest village, *where the water is colder than any other place in the Sahara. The boy's name is Moustapha.*

At noon, your truck struck a land mine, which had been buried there since World War II. *The Germans* had planted it there. The explosion was terrible, but fortunately no one was killed. However, the driver, *who has no health insurance,* was badly injured, and the physician says that he will die if he is not taken to a hospital. Also, the two assistants have suffered broken legs—*one the right leg, and the other the left leg*—and they cannot move. The truck, *a Mercedes,* is totally wrecked. But there is enough food *and water* to last nine days, provided that everyone stays quietly by the truck, *which is painted green.* Anyone leaving the truck would have to carry extra water *on his or her back* and thereby reduce the amount left for the others. You know that the police will begin to look for you.

Group II

You are on an *archaeological* expedition to the Sahara desert. The expedition members are as follows: Professor Jones, the 50-year-old leader, *who used to be a navy pilot;* William S. Benway, *whose hobby is gardening;* two assistants, *who are unmarried;* and a driver who is 34 years old *and used to race motorcycles.*

A few days ago, on *Tuesday,* you met a group of bedouin and agreed to take a woman who is pregnant and her two children, *a boy* aged 12 and *a girl* aged 13, to the nearest village.

At *exactly 12:15 P.M.,* your truck struck a land mine, which had been buried there since World War II. *The English* had planted it there. The explosion was terrible, but fortunately no one was killed. However, the driver, *who is left handed,* was badly injured, and the physician says that he will die if he is not taken to a hospital *within four days. Fortunately, his left arm was uninjured.* Also, the two assistants have suffered broken legs, and they cannot move. The truck is totally wrecked *and needed an oil change anyway.* But there is enough food to last nine days, provided that everyone stays quietly by the truck. *The assistants believe in astrology, and the moon is in Saturn.* Anyone leaving the truck would have to carry extra water and thereby reduce the amount left for the others. You know that the police will begin to look for you *if you do not report to the next town within seven days. And your sister, who works for the U.N., will also wonder what has happened to you.*

Commentary

The vocabulary here is not difficult, and the idea is that students will explain to each other the words they do not know. If the group has any doubts, you should help them. The only crucial and difficult words are "land mine" and "mine field." Students should decide for themselves whether these are personnel mines or tank/vehicular mines. They should note that the boundaries of the mine field are necessarily vague and not posted, and that the truck was destroyed by a mine outside of the mapped mine field. As you listen to the groups, you may bring up, if they do not, the difference between *astrology* and *astronomy*. When you hear an unchallenged irrelevancy, you might cough or in your own fashion signal distress to draw attention to it. Make sure that the students refer to the list of rejoinders to be used to point out irrelevancy.

Of critical importance is the discussion of how fast one can actually walk in the desert. Also, students will blithely volunteer to walk due north, but given where the accident took place, it is clear that the mine "field" extends beyond its markings. As for the oasis, bear in mind how easy it would be to miss such a small place thirty kilometers away. As for carrying water back from it, how is it to be carried? Water is very heavy. Almost as much would be used getting there and back as could be lugged.

Are there helicopters in small towns? Is there a compass? Would the camping equipment be intact? Is there food in an oasis? A McDonalds? These questions are best left to the group to decide, or guess, rather than the teacher providing a definitive yes or no. Some groups may come to quick decisions. In this case, after listening to their decision, you should bring up potential problems with it, then let them wrestle with it more thoroughly.

Health Care—Rationing

Time: Discussion of introductory questions and giving answers to social values questions, 10 min.

Part 1. Values That Affect Health Care Rationing

d   ability to function normally
a   cost-effectiveness or cost-ineffectiveness
c   length of life
f   quality of life
b   benefit to many as opposed to a few
e   equality of service

Part 3. Ranking Treatments as a Part of Health Care Rationing
Time: Discussion of question a or b: 5 min. Small group consensus, 40–60 min.

Health Care—Providing Services to Visible and Invisible Victims

Time: 30–50 min.

Knowledge, Information, and Ethics in Relation to Insurance and Health Care

Time: 20–30 min.

3. Psychology

Survey

Time: 15–20 min.
Answers

1. a
2. a
3. b
4. Women—usually better at reading facial expressions. Men—usually better at interpreting tone of voice.
5. a
6. no
7. Early in marriage: money, jealousy, relatives, communication, sex
   Parenthood: money, sex, jealousy, communication, relatives
   Later: money, sex, communication, relatives, jealousy
8. a
9. b

With question 6, you should ask the students which item they thought was first, second, and so forth, writing the order on the board as you hear it. You can play with suspense here. Note that money is always in first place. Ask why jealousy moves from second place early in marriage to third then to last place as time goes by. Ask why *sex* moves from last place in early marriage to second place during parenting. I have never had a problem with students addressing this question in a mature fashion. You also might ask why *relatives* are more of a problem early in marriage. This case allows you to call on the married poeple in your class as "experts."

Marriage, Cross-Culturally

Part 1. Marriage Is About
Time: 15 min.
Part 2. Characteristics of a Good Spouse
Time: 35–40 min.
In this section you may get some strange suggestions, and it does no good to have on the list items that virtually everyone will think inapplicable, so you should help the students whittle their lists. If you want a shortcut, here is a list that has been created after many "goes" at it.

Characteristics of a Good Spouse
kind
generous
healthy
intelligent
good lover
tolerant
forgiving
obedient
faithful
good sense of humor
physically attractive
loving
shared interests and tastes
shared political beliefs
supportive in bad times (*e.g., when money is tight, someone is very sick, etc.*)

Gender Attitudes

Time: 40–60 min.
Answers to Reading Questions: 1. b 2. b 3. b 4. b 5. c 6. a 7. a
The "Gender and Power in Discussion" exercise is often more difficult than it seems. Second language students often find it hard to decide what a challenge is or even what an interruption is. Therefore, the students chosen to quantify these indicators may not find this an easy task. Also, you may be surprised at the results. The goal here is neither accuracy nor orthodoxy but merely getting students sensitized to language and allowing them to see how fascinating it can be. Of course, another goal is getting them to understand that there are power issues at play in any communication.

Consider the oft-noted phenomenon that men tend not to be able to ask for directions when lost. (Some male comedians, for example, self-deprecatingly point this out for laughs.) You might ask your students if this is true in their cultures. And ask if women in those cultures, like American women, tend not to display this behavior.

Tag questions can also be confirmation-beggars, not real questions (e.g., "Nixon really was a crook, wasn't he[?]"). These, in my view, are expressions of power, but you need not complicate the task for the students since this kind of tag will seldom if ever be used by students. If you notice some of this sophisticated language use, you can talk about it after, or during, the class discussion of the results. It will be fascinating.

Marital Issues

Time: 40–60 min.

Divorce

Time: 30–45 min.

After a class discussion of the introductory question on fault as a determinant in awarding alimony, the teacher should read the three scenarios of the Joneses. Get several responses, enough to show real differences of opinion and arouse interest, but with no discussion.

When the groups have finished, write their decisions for the three cases on the chalkboard. Now you can draw conclusions about the justice of treating *fault* for men and for women. Case *a* is the baseline. A nonsexist decision will vary in case *b* and case *c by the same amount!* For example, if the alimony in case *a* is $10,000, in case *b* is $15,000, and in case *c* is $5,000, then the *fault* is penalized by $5,000 in cases *b* and *c*.

The same variance from the baseline will probably occur about 33% of the time. Most of the time, however, you will find that fault for the woman is penalized much more than fault for the man. Some students will justify this result by citing that the man brings in the money, or at least the lion's share of it. If this is the case, then the woman does not have equal rights to the distribution thereof.

I tend to let the facts speak for themselves. The seeds of doubt will be sown in the minds of some students. When social values are deeply ingrained, this is probably the best one can do. If students are to revise their values, the impetus must come from within. I think you will find that you have sown a robust seed.

Rationality (Sunk Costs)

Time: 90 min.–2 hrs.

N.B.: This is a presentation exercise (that is, individual students will present reports to the class) and the *Peer Feedback Sheet* (that appears in chapter 7) should be photocopied and used. Do not be daunted by the time needed. You can do two cases per day. Even if you have a two-hour class, it is not advisable to do all in one day. If you have videotaping capability, this is a good time to use it both for individual presentation and for class discussion. Another variation is possible if the environment is such that asking people their opinions outside of class is not feasible: you can have students learn to present one question, without looking at the other questions. Then have them ask each other their questions in class, roving around and telling their particular scenario to others who do not have the same case to present. After one student explains his or her hypothetical situation and elicits an opinion, the other does the same.

Experiments 1 and 2 present clear cases of sunk costs. Would you go where you would prefer not to be just because you already had paid for that privilege? You should feel free to share your own point of view, but console those who honor the sunk costs by pointing out that many of the American subjects in the original experiments also did so. Leave open the possibility of differing versions of rationality.

Experiments 3 and 4 show two sides of the same coin. There seems little economic reason to complete the project in either case. It would result in a loss. Students will suggest that they will sell their plane more cheaply, but you should point out that the competition can cut costs and be in the black while you are in the red. Those who chose *yes* in 3 are honoring a sunk cost, which seems irrational, but the vast majority of subjects in the original experiments chose *yes*. Again, however, it is irrational to be contradictory, and those who chose *yes* for 3 and *no* for 4 appear to be acting contradictorily. Some Japanese students have pointed out that *yes* is the appropriate answer for both and that Americans who choose *no* are following the typical American business pattern of looking at short-run profit. Sometimes, the Japanese say, you have to take a loss just to get market share, to get your name out there. What you learn from this mistake may come in handy in your next venture. This is an interesting argument.

In experiment 5 the loss of $10 is not linked specifically to the ticket purchase, and its effect on the decision accordingly is slight. In experiment 6 the expense to see the show was seen as $20, a cost that many of the respondents apparently found excessive. To be rational, one cannot be contradictory. It is difficult to defend the rationality of choosing *yes* in one of these two experiments and *no* in the other. Some students will not see the play because they will not enjoy it, thinking all the while of where they might have lost the ticket or the money, but this sentiment should apply to both 5 and 6.

It is interesting to note that self-punishment is sometimes the rationale for not buying another ticket. This appears to be at odds with the economists' notion of a rational person, all of whose actions are motivated by self-interest. It is curious to consider how self-punishment can be self-interest.

Synergy (Lost at Sea)

Time: 50 min. at least for discussion, 15 min. more the following day for synergy report

Manage the time carefully if you need to finish the discussion and the giving of the answers within your time limit. Push any group that is behind the others. When assigning this the day before, for homework, get a volunteer to do the synergy report and let him or her read the directions carefully. You should allow the student some time with you to answer any question he or she has. This is really *not* complicated. All students will understand it. You just need to spend 15 minutes yourself to figure it out.

Also, try to go over the list of items in class. Ask if there are any that the students don't understand, and let other students explain the vocabulary. Usually, they can. For example, "mosquito netting" is not always universally understood.

Answers

According to the experts, the basic supplies needed when a person is stranded in the midocean are articles to attract attention and articles to aid survival until rescuers arrive. Articles for navigation are of little importance: even if a small life raft were capable of reaching land, it would be impossible to store enough food and water to subsist during that period of time. Therefore, of primary importance are the shaving mirror and the two-gallon can of oil-gas mixture. These items could be used for signaling air-sea rescue. Of secondary importance are items such as water and food, for example, the case of emergency food.

The rationale for the ranking of the items that follows does not represent all of the potential uses for the specified items but, rather, the primary importance of each.

1. shaving mirror—critical for signaling air-sea rescue

2. two-gallon can of oil-gas mixture—critical for signaling (the mixture will float on the water and could be ignited with a dollar bill and a match— obviously outside the raft)

3. five-gallon can of water

4. one case (24 cans) emergency food

5. 20 square feet of opaque plastic—to collect rain water and for shelter from elements

6. two boxes of chocolate bars—reserve food supply

7. fishing kit—ranked lower than the candy bars because "a bird in the hand is worth two in the bush" (there is no assurance that you will catch any fish)

8. fifteen feet of nylon rope—to tie equipment down and prevent it from falling overboard

9. Seat cushion (flotation device)—life preserver if anyone were to fall overboard

10. shark repellent—obvious

11. one quart of strong rum, 80% alcohol (that is, 160 proof)—antiseptic

12. one "Walkman" radio—has no transmitter and you're out of range of your favorite station

13. maps of the Pacific Ocean—worthless without additional navigational equipment

14. mosquito netting—no mosquitoes in the mid Pacific

15. sextant—without tables and chronometer (stopwatch), relatively useless (alternatively, hit the shark with it. . . or the guy who is drinking your share of the rum)

4. Philosophy (Distributive Justice)

All these cases are intermediate level material that can be used at the advanced level. Since these cases treat the same general issue, it is advisable not to do all of them. I find that "The Candy Bar Dilemma" is a good "first day" exercise that can be done for fun (with candy as a prize) at low advanced levels. The cases can also be given as dictation. For long cases, you might do just one paragraph as dictation.

The Candy Bar Dilemma

Time: 30 min.
Deceptively simple, this case deals with all the criteria for a just distribution: *want, need,* and *desert.* This case is difficult because all of them want the candy (you cannot let the teens make the decision—they will fight—and you cannot

buy another bar), but none of them needs it. (*N.B.:* It may seem strange to include "want" as a criterion, but absent claims of need or desert, it is just to distribute a good on the basis of who wants it.) The question here is "who needs most *not* to have it." And the importance of teaching Carol not to be a pig should not be undervalued. You should begin by getting suggestions for as many different distributions as possible and writing them on the board. Then challenge students individually ("Do you agree with this one?"). The writing on this seemingly superficial but actually profound topic can be very good. And there are built-in organizational units. You will need to have available two candy bars for each small group.

The Race

Time: 30–50 min.
The issue dealt with here is also valuable at an advanced level. In *The Race*, we are faced with the ultimate question of validity of any *criterion* in a just distribution. (Thus, this case follows, perhaps dovetails with, *The Candy Bar* case.) The distribution is of an honor—making the track team.

The major criterion at work here is *desert*. (Note, however, that the claims of Carlos and Ben are largely based on *want* and *need*, respectively.) Ordinarily, one makes the team not by wanting or needing but by deserving. (Isn't Ben's claim a form of blackmail?)

But it seems that no single criterion is ever valid for justice. The context is all important. There does not seem to be any criterion that should not, in some case, be amended. This is one of the primary bases for affirmative action. Desert is not so cut and dried as we often think.

Intuitively, we all have criteria for desert. One of these, universally recognized, is responsibility. Students will pick up on this, especially in the case of Harry. But the waters (or perhaps the track) soon become muddy, for some will feel that a person is responsible for catching a cold while others will find this more an accident of nature.

Political philosopher William Galston's conclusion of like issues is that *there is no criterion that cannot be bent*. But if we can bend the rules justly in one case, why not in another, and another—so that here the qualification race is interminable. In effect, we decide where to draw the line *arbitrarily* within some societal consensus. This has ramifications for affirmative action, admission to schools, etc.

Mrs. Kerr and Ms. Pink

Part 1
Time: 20 min.

Part 2
Time: 20 min.
Instruct presenters to learn the case and retell it. They should not try to memorize it.

You need not do both parts. If you do both, Part 2 needs to be done on another day, as the roles must be learned.

Finders, Keepers

Time: 30 min.
The case may be done as *presentation*. It is best if you decide on some maximum number of the items to be distributed, smaller than the number of group members. Otherwise, the decision becomes easy—everyone gets one. You should feel free to veto any suggestions for additional items that you think unsuitable—for example, "my boyfriend." And you will get some funny and outrageous ones, like "an inflatable replica of my boyfriend."

Joe, His Bread, the Lifeboat

Time: 30 min.
The case may be done as *presentation*. One student may be asked to present the case to the students, with the briefest of notes, if any.

A follow-up to this unit that some teachers have found fitting is watching Alfred Hitchcock's *Lifeboat*.

Sam and the Posse

Time: 30 min.
The case may be done as *presentation*. One student may be asked to present the case to the students, with the briefest of notes, if any.

5. Law

Crime and Punishment

Time: 50–70 min.
Teacher may play devil's advocate to get things going if there is general agreement. Get two or three opinions on some of the topics before doing small group work. Repeat the procedural instruction to try to recall similar scenarios that the students might know of and give them an opportunity to talk about these incidents in class.

Question 1.   You may help by giving students the term *attempted murder.*
Question 3.   The man's actions (you can act it out) make it appear that he clearly
               had the *intention* to kill. But as we can see, although murder is
               defined by intention, this term is very slippery.
Question 4.   With more detailed cases like this one it is often useful to ask some
               students to recap.
Question 6.   "Private punishment" is the theme. In European law, private pun-
               ishment is acceptable in the very rare case when the wrongdoer
               cannot be brought to justice *and* the punisher is certain of the guilt
               of the malefactor. Here, Edwina isn't saving anyone by slitting the
               parachute. She is planning the death of Patty.
Question 9.   This is fun to act out.

Humor in the Court

Time: 10–15 min.
This can be done in small groups or by the class as a whole.

The Case of Humbert Phillips

Time: Discussion questions, 50–60 min. Trial, 50–60 min.
"Harmless wrong" refers to things like not paying taxes (no physical harm).
"Wrongless harm" refers, for example, to a virus: it harms but cannot be said to
be doing any wrong. As I see it, in the political philosophy of liberalism (cf. Joel
Fineberg), harm is the critical ingredient in deciding what punishment should
be. A more Aristotelian approach would be to take into consideration a
malefactor's character. Herein is justification for more severe punishment for
the loathsome individual with a long track record of malfeasance and less severe
punishment for individuals with outstanding character and records of public service.

Of special interest in this case are the notion of blackmail and the question
of whether or not you can blackmail someone into doing good. If you thus *coerce* someone into doing good, is it still blackmail? If this is considered blackmail, then it would seem to fall into the category of harmless wrong.

Similarly, putting an ad in the paper offering a prize (money) for anyone who
can climb Mt. Everest might be seen as a wrongless harm, since it can hardly be
against the law, but the person who places the ad must know that desperate
people will be harmed, perhaps killed, trying to win the prize money.

And nude sunbathing may be seen as a harmless (moral) wrong by some but
as a wrongless harm by others—if it is legal.

Those of you intrigued by this unit may want to look at *Trial by Jury,* Kevin
King, Newbury House, 1984. *The Case of Humbert Phillips* follows the same
format used there.

6. Linguistics

You Don't Understand Me

Time: 40 min.

Cross-Cultural and Paralinguistic Exercise: In a multicultural class, ask two students to take their chairs to the front of the room and act out (reading, if they want) one or more of the scenarios. Make note of the positioning of the chairs. Are they facing each other? How close are they? I had one phenomenally illustrative class where one student kept dragging his chair back as the other dragged his forward, "encroaching." This only stopped when the former reached the wall. After having several pairs do this, ask the class if they remember how any of the pairs stationed themselves, and ask what this tells about comfort zones.

Exercise 1. Carla was annoyed, not because she had not gotten her way, but because her preference had not been considered. She had wanted some popcorn. Rhett feels that people should say what they want, that Carla's manner is a kind of game playing.

Exercise 2. Cordelia is irritated because she thought that Henry was withholding part of his life from her. She wants to offer emotional support, which he feels he doesn't need, since men are brought up to ignore minor injuries.

Exercise 3. Prospero provides information other than that which Miranda requests. His reason (regarding the quantity of wine) *may be* that he is being protective of her. She may think that his replies show that he is on a power trip. One term used for this kind of response is mind reading. This can be offensive and presumptuous. It also is consistent with trying to hold power in a relationship.

Exercise 4. This is very typical—men want to solve problems and women want to give and get empathy, emotional support. Anthony is happy with his ability to give Clea advice, but Clea thinks that he doesn't understand what she is feeling.

Exercise 5. Orson doesn't understand that Marilyn's question is a suggestion.

Exercise 6. Rhett doesn't understand that Carla's questions are an indirect way of saying she'd rather see some other movie. And Carla doesn't care so much about the popcorn as she does about sharing. Rhett does not understand this need.

Arranging the Marriage of Indira and Raphael (An Indirect Speech Exercise)

Time: 1 hr.

Tell Raphael's family the following rumors. It is said that Indira has a very bad temper that she does not try to control. (Consider, also, the possibility of using these rumors: (1) She is a radical feminist who hates men; (2) She is not a virgin.) It is said that she plans to have thirty-seven cats as soon as she has a home of her own. It is said that she is allergic to some very common substances like cotton.

Tell Indira's family the following rumors. It is said that there is a history of insanity in Raphael's family. It is said that Raphael loves garlic and must have it with every meal and that his breath smells bad. It is also said that he hates children and small furry animals.

Conditionally Speaking

Time: 30–40 min.

1. No. There might be French donkeys in Spain, in which case the donkey in *a* is beaten but the donkey in *b* is not.
2. Yes
3. False. A black-eyed donkey might be both stubborn and stupid.
4. Yes! In *b* you *must* open it to prevent the explosion! *N.B.:* The word "then" does not usually have this force. But what *b* means is "if and only if" or "provided that."
5. The butler is not the murderer. This can be fun. If you are familiar with logical notation and transitivity theory, you might find the following proof valuable. For most teachers, however, this proof will be superfluous.

   P = Butler is murderer   Q = Butler left by window   R = Butler has mud on shoes.
   P $\rightarrow$ Q   Q $\rightarrow$ R , therefore P $\rightarrow$ R
   P $\rightarrow$ R
       $-$R
       _____
       $-$P

6. a. Speaker is a teacher. Listener is a bad student and speech act is an incentive *or* listener is a good student and the speech act is a threat.
   b. Speaker is a teacher. Listener is a good student. Speech act is a threat.

N.B.: The important thing to note is that conditionals do not need an *if*. This kind of conditional is common in spoken English.

7. Business Negotiation

Freeloaders

Time: 30–40 min.

The Great Bun Caper
Time: Presentation of case and game, 20–25 min. Filling out feedback sheets and oral feedback, 10 min. Negotiation game, 30 min.

The Cow Dung Gaffe

Time: Presentation of case and game, 20–25 min. Filling out feedback sheets and oral feedback, 10 min. Negotiation game, 20–30 min.

The Great Bun Caper and *The Cow Dung Gaffe* are cases for presentation. The teacher will need to meet with the presenters in *The Great Bun Caper* prior to class to assist them with their preparation. The presentations may be videotaped and replayed in the next class with appropriate analysis. It is, in my experience, not a wise allocation of time to replay all of a long presentation. Five minutes replay should be sufficient for each presenter.

After the case is done, students must fill out *Peer Feedback Sheets* (a reproducible sheet follows *The Cow Dung Gaffe* section in this chapter) on both the case and game presenters. If all is not done on the same day, feedback should be collected on the first day for the first presenter. These sheets are collected by the teacher and given to the presenter. It is often helpful to get some oral feedback, and the first comments should be positive. If you thought that students did something particularly well, ask for oral comments on that aspect of the presentation. The presenters then must write one paragraph on "What I Can Do to Improve Next Time."

These cases involve negotiation games. The value of such games is very well documented. Students presenting this, and other demanding cases, might be awarded special compensation if yours is a class in which grades are given.

Laying Off at the Auto Plant (A Personnel Dilemma)
Time: 30 min.